The Rehabilitation of Offenders: A Guide to the Law

Fourmat Publishing

The Rehabilitation of Offenders: A Guide to the Law

by Brian Harris, OBE, QC, LL.B

Second edition

London
Fourmat Publishing
1988

ISBN 1 85190 057 8

First published in 1976 by Barry Rose Publishers Ltd
This edition 1988

27 & 28 St Albans Place Islington Green London N1 0NX

Printed in Great Britain by
Billing & Sons Limited, Worcester

Preface

From its inception, the Rehabilitation of Offenders Act was a controversial measure, as may be seen from the historical note at Appendix 5.

Theoretically, the Act should have had a major impact on the treatment, in court and out, of an offender's record. Despite this fact and the extraordinarily complex nature of its hastily drafted provisions, the Act has given rise to very little in the way of case law.

From the outset, those with responsibility for the protection of the public have realised that the Act was not to be trusted. The outward and visible manifestation of this feeling is the Exceptions Order of 1975. Since the first edition the scope of this Order has been considerably extended by later Orders (Appendix 2). Recent legislation in the field of banking and financial legislation has resulted in further, but regrettably different, exceptions now discussed at pages 44–45.

I draw attention at pages 12–13 to the doubts which surround the application of the Act to what are two of the commonest orders made in criminal proceedings, namely the order of endorsement of a driving licence and the order of costs against a convicted defendant. Both cry out for amendment.

It really is time that someone got hold of this well intentioned but quite hopeless legislation and replaced it by something simpler, more honest and more effective. I hope I do not have to prepare a third edition.

Brian Harris
June 1988

Acknowledgements

I am grateful to the Home Office and Her Majesty's Stationery Office for permission to reproduce some of the examples from their circular and booklet respectively.

Contents

Table of Cases

Chapter 1

The Act in outline

The basic principle of the Act enshrined in s 1 (1) is that, following a certain period of time, which depends on the sentence imposed (see Chapter 3) and may be extended by the subsequent criminal career of the offender (Chapters 4 and 5), all convictions except those resulting in long prison sentences are regarded as "spent" and the offender a "rehabilitated person."

A rehabilitated person is treated as a person who has not committed or been charged with or prosecuted for or convicted of or sentenced for the offence: s 4(1). The Act does not rely on the lawyer's construction of this statement, which might otherwise be thought broad and clear enough for most purposes, but goes on to spell out specific immunities and privileges attaching to the concept of rehabilitation.

Thus, a rehabilitated person is entitled to ignore spent convictions in reply to questions about his past, whether put to him in court (Chapter 6) or out (Chapter 9), and the existence of a spent conviction should not prejudice him in getting or keeping a job (Chapter 9). To these rules there are many exceptions. Most notably, the Act has no application to criminal proceedings (Chapter 8) except to the extent to which a Practice Direction of the Lord Chief Justice requires its spirit to be observed. Nor does it apply to certain civil proceedings (Chapter 7), and certain occupations and activities have been exempted by Ministerial order (Chapter 10).

There are both civil and criminal sanctions against the unlawful dissemination of spent convictions. First, a malicious reference to a spent conviction can give rise to an action for damages (Chapter 11). Secondly, it is a criminal offence to disclose a spent conviction from official records otherwise than in the course of official duties. Lastly, it is an offence corruptly to obtain details of a spent conviction (Chapter 12).

The text of the Act is contained in Appendix 1. It does not apply to Northern Ireland: s 11(3).

Chapter 2

The scope of the Act

1. "Conviction" widely defined

The Act's protection applies to all convictions, save those which result in an excluded sentence (see page 6 below). Since the term "conviction" has a narrow and precise meaning in the criminal law, the ambit of the Act is considerably extended by enlarging it to include *any finding in criminal proceedings other than one linked with a finding of insanity:* s 1(4). This is not an exhaustive but only a partial definition of the term "conviction" which must therefore continue to bear its ordinary meaning and cannot, for example, extend to acquittals, dismissals or discharges (which can never be described as convictions), although mention of an acquittal can sometimes do as much harm as mention of a conviction.

It was said by Viscount Cave in *Re Clifford & O'Sullivan* (1921) that a criminal cause or matter must involve the consideration of some charge of crime, that is to say of an offence against the public law, and a claim to criminal jurisdiction. In *R* v *Army Council, ex parte Sandford* (1940) it was suggested that this extends to matters affecting the exercise of criminal jurisdiction, such as applications for a prerogative order of mandamus, certiorari or prohibition. The fact that proceedings are heard in a criminal court does not affix them with a criminal character. It must be doubted, for example, whether the Act extends to bind-over proceedings, whether following an arrest at common law or on a complaint under the Magistrates' Courts Act 1980, s 115(1). It would apply, however, to a bind-over made as, or as part of, a sentence.

The exclusion of findings linked with insanity is clearly

intended to deal with verdicts of not guilty by reason of insanity under the Criminal Procedure (Insanity) Act 1974 and its predecessor Act of 1833, but not a finding of diminished responsibility under the Homicide Act 1957. A finding that the accused did the act or made the omission charged in accordance with the Mental Health Act 1983 s 27(3) is a conviction attracting rehabilitation within the meaning of s 1(4) of the 1974 Act.

The Act is specifically applied to findings in the course of care proceedings that a juvenile has committed an offence or done the act or made the omission charged: s 1(4). Corresponding provision is made by s 3 for findings at children's hearings in Scotland.

An offence for which a probation order or an order of absolute or conditional discharge is made is deemed not to be a conviction for most purposes by the Powers of Criminal Courts Act 1973, s 13, and this rule is unaffected by the Rehabilitation of Offenders Act. However, in order to ensure that the additional protection which the 1974 Act affords may be extended to such orders, it is provided in s 1(4) that, notwithstanding the 1973 Act, they shall be deemed to be convictions which may be the subject of rehabilitation.

2. Foreign convictions

The Act applies not only to convictions in this country, but also to convictions before courts outside Great Britain: s 1(4). The foreign sentence (and this includes a Northern Ireland conviction) is to be treated as equivalent to the English sentence which most nearly corresponds to it: s 5(9).

This recognition of foreign convictions should not be confused with the operation of the Act, which does not extend beyond Great Britain (see page 42.)

3. Date of conviction

The Act applies to all convictions whenever they occurred. Any conviction which under the Act would otherwise have become spent before the date of coming into force of the Act (1 July 1975) is treated as having become spent on that date: s 1(1).

Examples

(a) On 15 March 1965 a man was convicted of receiving stolen goods and sent to prison for three months. The rehabilitation period is seven years and therefore ran out on 15 March 1972. But the Act did not come into force until 1 July 1975, and so he became a rehabilitated person and the conviction became spent on that day, provided he was not convicted again before then of an indictable offence. But if the rehabilitation period had not run out before 1 July 1975, he would have had to wait until it did.

(b) On 21 June 1971 a man was convicted of shoplifting and fined £25. The rehabilitation period is five years, and the conviction becomes spent on 21 June 1976 (by which time the Act is in force) provided he is not convicted again before then of an indictable offence.

4. Living people alone protected

The concept of rehabilitation applies only to people not to other legal persons such as limited companies; at least this would appear to be the implication of the use of the term "individual" in s 1(1). However, certain provisions of the Act, for example s 4(3)(a) which relieves persons of any legal obligation to disclose spent convictions, are wide enough to include companies.

The Act works mainly to protect the living. The criminal offences created by s 9 are restricted to disclosures affecting living persons, and it is not in general a ground of action to defame the dead.

5. Royal pardon

The Act does not affect the Royal prerogative of mercy or

the right to commute sentence: s 7(1)(a). A pardon does not expunge a conviction but a pardoned conviction is capable of becoming spent: s 4(1).

6. Disqualifications, prohibitions and penalties

The fact that a person has been convicted of a particular offence may render him subject to a disqualification, prohibition or disability by operation of law quite apart from any order of the court.
Examples are:

- automatic suspension of a driving licence when the licence is not produced to the court on conviction of an endorseable offence: Road Traffic Act 1972, s 101(4);
- prohibition of possessing firearms by offenders who have received certain sentences: Firearms Act 1968, s 21.

Nothing in the Act affects the exercise of these or similar provisions: s 7(1)(d).

7. Excluded sentences

Certain sentences are excluded altogether from any possibility of rehabilitation by ss 1(1) and 5. They are:

- life imprisonment;
- imprisonment, youth custody (or the former sentence of corrective training) for a term exceeding 30 months;
- (the former sentence of) preventive detention;
- detention during Her Majesty's pleasure for life, or under s 205(2) or (3) of the Criminal Procedure (Scotland) Act 1975, or for a term exceeding 30 months under s 53 of the Children and Young Persons Act 1933, or under s 206 of the Criminal Procedure (Scotland) Act 1975 or a corresponding court martial punishment; and
- a sentence of custody for life.

A conviction resulting in any of these sentences can never become spent, nor does any other provision of the Act apply to it. Furthermore, as will be seen later (see page 19) the commission of an offence resulting in an excluded sentence (as they are called) acts to prevent any earlier unspent conviction from becoming spent.

Chapter 3

Rehabilitation periods

Except for the excluded sentences (page 6) the Act provides a separate rehabilitation period for every sentence. "Sentence" is defined in s 1(3) as including *any order made by a court in dealing with a person in respect of his conviction* except:

(a) committals to prison for non-payment of fines, etc; and

(b) orders dealing with a person in respect of a suspended sentence of imprisonment.

For further consideration of this term see page 12.

The length of the rehabilitation period appropriate to each sentence is defined in s 5 of the Act. The effect of that section on the principal sentences is summarized in the following table. In each case where a fixed period of years is shown in the right-hand column this runs from the date of conviction and not the date of the offence. Sometimes a court will postpone sentence for a period after conviction; if so, the rehabilitation period still seemingly starts from the earlier, not the later, date. Certain periods are reduced by half where the offender was under seventeen years of age at the date of conviction.

Sentence	*Rehabilitation period*
A sentence of imprisonment or youth custody of more than 6 months but not more than 30 months	10 years for an adult, 5 for a juvenile.
A sentence of imprisonment or youth custody of 6 months or less.	7 years for an adult, 5 for a juvenile.

An order of detention in a detention centre.	3 years.
A fine	5 years for an adult, 2½ for a juvenile.
A community service order.	5 years for an adult.
Probation, bind-over to keep the peace or be of good behaviour, and conditional discharge.	The date the order or bind-over ceases or one year, whichever is the longer.
Care and supervision orders under the Children and Young Persons Acts.	The date the order ceases or one year, whichever is the longer.
Attendance centre orders.	1 year after the order expires.
Hospital orders under the Mental Health Act 1983.	5 years from the date of conviction or two years after the order expires, whichever is the longer.
Disqualification and other orders imposing disability, prohibition or other penalty.	The date the order ceases to have effect. (see page 12)
Absolute discharge.	6 months.

1. Servicemen

The Act applies to findings of guilt in service disciplinary proceedings where the conduct amounts to:

(a) a civil offence; or
(b) any one of certain specified military offences; or
(c) any other military offence which results in detention for three months or more or any more serious punishment.

s 2(1)-(4).

The rehabilitation periods for imprisonment in the armed services are the same as for those in the civil courts. Any sentence of detention arising from service disciplinary proceedings carries a rehabilitation period of five years. For discharge with ignominy, dismissal with disgrace and the obsolete sentence of cashiering the period is ten years and, for dismissal from the service, seven. All periods are reduced by half if the offender is under seventeen at the time of conviction. Less serious offences, such as failing to salute an officer, are not affected unless a sentence of detention of three months or more is imposed.

2. Suspended sentences

At law, a suspended prison sentence is as much a sentence of imprisonment as one that takes effect forthwith and the periods of rehabilitation are therefore the same. In the case of a partly suspended sentence it is the total period of the sentence (ie the suspended and forthwith elements added together) which determines the length of the sentence.

One of the possible courses open to the court when putting a suspended sentence into effect is to order that it take effect with a lesser term substituted for that originally fixed. The Act provides that this variation of term is to be ignored in determining the rehabilitation period to be applied to the original sentence: s 5(9)(c).

Example

If a nine-month suspended sentence is later put into effect as a six-month sentence it still attracts the longer rehabilitation period of ten years appropriate to the original sentence rather than the shorter period of seven years appropriate to the sentence actually served.

The sentence imposed for the later conviction may affect the rehabilitation period for the suspended sentence under the terms of s 6(4) of the Act (see Chapter 5). And this applies whether the suspended sentence is put into effect or not. Putting a suspended sentence of imprisonment into effect does not count as a separate sentence so as to attract a separate rehabilitation period: s 1(3).

3. Consecutive sentences

Where an offender receives two or more prison sentences in the course of the same proceedings the Act provides that the terms shall be aggregated, either concurrently or consecutively according to the order of the court, so as to be treated as a single term: s 5(9)(b).

> *Example*
>
> Two six-month terms ordered to take effect consecutively are treated as a single term of twelve months, giving each conviction a rehabilitation period of ten years, but two such sentences ordered to take effect concurrently are treated as one sentence of six months, giving each conviction a rehabilitation period of seven years.

Sometimes, the effect of this can be to exclude convictions altogether from the possibility or rehabilitation, for example where two two-year sentences are ordered to take effect consecutively and become a single term of four years.

Prison sentences ordered to take effect consecutively to sentences already being served are not affected by this rule.

The aggregation of consecutive sentences (s 5(9)(b)) has not been applied to sentences of youth custody (possibly by an oversight). The effect of this is that two or more consecutive sentences of youth custody which are individually less than 30 months in duration, but in total exceed 30 months, will nevertheless attract rehabilitation.

4. Multiple sentences

It is often possible for an offender to receive more than one sentence for a single offence. The Act provides that in such cases the rehabilitation period is the longest of those applicable: s 6(2).

> *Example*
>
> For the same offence a person is fined £50 and sentenced to one month's imprisonment. The

rehabilitation period is seven years (see the table on page 8).

This rule also applies to probationers subsequently sentenced for the original offence. See pages 21–22.

Section 6(2) will catch the situation where an offender is sentenced to imprisonment and a fine; it does not deal with the fixing of a term of imprisonment to be served in default of payment of a fine (which is provided for by s 1(3) of the Act): *Arif v Excess Insurance Co Ltd* (1982).

5. Disqualification and other ancillary orders

Apart from sentences properly so called, an offender may be the subject of a number of ancillary orders, for example, disqualification, compensation and forfeiture. By defining a sentence as including any order made by a court in dealing with a person in connexion with any offence (s 1(3)) the Act treats each of these orders as a sentence with a separate rehabilitation period under s 5. This in turn attracts the rule in s 6(2) that the rehabilitation period is the longest of those applicable.

Example:

On 20 November 1983, someone is convicted of reckless driving, fined £100 and disqualified for seven years. If he is not convicted again, the conviction becomes spent on 20 November 1990, not 20 November 1988 (see table on page 8).

An order for costs would paradoxically appear to fall within the definition of a "sentence" in s 1(3) of the Act, although it seems undesirable for such an ancillary order to have, under Table A of s 5 of the Act, a rehabilitation period (five years for an adult) which could easily be longer than the sentence properly so called. It is also suggested that a recommendation for deportation under s 6 of the Immigration Act 1971 does not constitute a sentence for the purposes of this Act.

6. Endorsement

Strangely enough, there is room for doubt as to the

rehabilitation period applicable to one of the most commonly made orders on conviction, namely an order under s 101 of the Road Traffic Act 1972 that an offender's driving licence shall be endorsed. (It should be noted that the endorsement of a licence as a result of a fixed penalty is treated for the purposes of the 1974 Act in exactly the same way as an endorsement ordered upon conviction: see Transport Act 1982, s 34(7)).

Such an order is clearly a sentence within the meaning of s 1(3) of the 1974 Act. Where, as will be the case whenever a disqualification is not imposed, the order of endorsement is accompanied by an order under s 19 of the Transport Act 1981 that a number of penalty points should be included in the particulars endorsed on the licence, the question arises whether this constitutes "an order imposing a disqualification, disability, prohibition or other penalty" so as to attract s 5(8) of the 1974 Act. If it does, then the period of rehabilitation is four years in the ordinary case under s 101(7A) of the Road Traffic Act 1972, or eleven years in the case of a conviction related to drunken driving. An order to endorse penalty points is clearly not a disqualification or prohibition and almost certainly not a disability; the question remaining is whether it is a penalty.

While the point is not free from doubt, it is suggested that the order to endorse penalty points is not in itself a penalty, but merely an order which could at some future date, and in the event of future acts, attract an order of disqualification. If this view is correct, it follows that the rehabilitation period appropriate to an endorsement accompanied by penalty points is five years (three for a juvenile) in accordance with Table A of Section 5 of the 1974 Act. This would seem to be the case notwithstanding that the endorsement may have become ineffective earlier by virtue of s 101(7A) of the Road Traffic Act 1972. This amomalous state of affairs (like the situation regarding costs – see page 12) cries out for amending legislation.

7. A special exception

As will be explained (page 20), the period of rehabilitation appropriate to a disqualification, endorsement or any other prohibition or penalty is disregarded totally when it comes to assessing the effect of any subsequent conviction.

Chapter 4

Unserved sentences

A person who has not actually served his sentence cannot claim to have paid his debt to society and it would be illogical to describe him as rehabilitated. The Act accordingly provides in s 1(2) that *a rehabilitation period does not expire until the sentence has been served or otherwise undergone or complied with.* In the most obvious case this means that anyone who escapes from prison cannot count towards his rehabilitation period the time when he was at large. Presumably after recapture time recommences to run from the moment of his being lodged again in prison. It is suggested that a person discharged with remission of sentence has served his sentence, but not one released on parole.

1. Driving while disqualified

The act of driving while disqualified would not, it is suggested, be sufficient to delay the rehabilitation period of a disqualified driver, because the order of the court was not that the offender should not drive, but that he should be disqualified for holding or obtaining a driving licence. To drive while disqualified is an offence under the Road Traffic Act 1972, conviction of which may entail the quite separate consequences provided in ss 5 and 6 of the Rehabilitation of Offenders Act. It is suggested that the same principles apply to the act of obtaining a driving licence while disqualified, because a disqualification for obtaining a driving licence is not the same thing as an order forbidding the obtaining of such a licence.

The non-impeding effect of driving while disqualified

should not be confused with the rule regarding conviction for a further offence, under which a conviction for driving while disqualified may serve to extend the rehabilitation period of the original offence (see Chapter 5).

2. Exceptions

Because of the difficulties of knowing whether a person has actually served or complied with a sentence, and for other reasons, s 1(2) provides that the following shall not affect the running of the rehabilitation period:

(a) failure to pay a fine etc.

(b) breach of a recognizance to keep the peace or be of good behaviour;

(c) liability to be dealt with in respect of a suspended sentence;

(d) failure to comply with any requirement of a suspended sentence;

(e) supervision order; and

(f) breach of any condition or requirement of an order which renders a person liable to be dealt with for the original offence, for example, breach of a probation order, community service order, attendance centre order or order of conditional discharge.

It is important to distinguish these exceptions to the unserved-sentence rule from:

(a) the commission of a further offence during a probation order or the operational period of a suspended sentence, which carries its own rehabilitation period and may have an effect on the earlier period in accordance with s 6; and

(b) any punishment imposed for a breach of probation, whether as a penalty in its own right or in respect of the original offence.

(See Chapter 5.)

3. Enforcement proceedings

In order to allow effective action to be taken against those who fail to comply with the sentence of the court, it is provided that the restrictions of the Act shall not affect the enforcement of fines and similar sums or proceedings for breach of any condition or requirement of a sentence, such as breach of probation, estreatment of recognizances, etc: s 7(1).

Chapter 5

Committing further offences

The essence of rehabilitation is that the person who has been convicted does not offend again. Section 6(4) of the Act deals with this by providing that *the effect of a subsequent conviction during a period of rehabilitation for an offence is to extend whichever of the rehabilitation periods expires first until the expiry of the one which expires later.*

The Act speaks of a "further offence," and its effect would not appear to be confined to subsequent offences, ie offences *committed* after the date of the first conviction. To invoke the extension provisions of s 6(4) it is only necessary that the conviction, and not the offence, should take place within the rehabilitation period. A subsequent conviction for any offence committed prior to the original offence is as effective in invoking the extension provisions of s 6(4) as a subsequent conviction for a subsequent offence.

The combined effect of ss 1(4) and 6(4) of the Act is to ensure that even a further conviction resulting in a probation order or order of absolute or conditional discharge may extend the rehabilitation period of the earlier order, or be extended thereby, notwithstanding s 13 of the Powers of Criminal Courts Act 1973 under which such orders do not normally count as convictions.

1. Purely summary offences ignored

It would be unreasonable to apply the rule of extension to every offence, however trivial, and only those which can be tried on indictment have this effect, whether they are actually tried on indictment or not: s 6(6). If the later conviction is for an offence which is triable only summarily, that is to say an offence, like highway obstruction, which cannot be tried before a judge and jury, then the rehabilitation period for the first offence is not affected. Of course the purely summary offence will carry its own rehabilitation period, but this will not affect nor be affected by the rehabilitation period for the earlier conviction.

Example

On 17 September 1983, someone is convicted of assault, and sent to prison for one month. On 3 February 1986, he is convicted again, this time for stealing, and fined £50. The rehabilitation period for the first of these convictions is seven years; for the second it is five. But the longer one extends the shorter; if he is not convicted again, therefore, *both* these convictions become spent together on 3 February 1991. But if the second conviction is for speeding (which can only be tried in a magistrates' court in England and Wales, and in Scotland is not excluded from the jurisdiction of inferior courts of summary jurisdiction) it cannot extend the rehabilitation period which is still running. The first conviction therefore becomes spent on 17 September 1990, and the second on 3 February 1991.

2. Foreign offences

The further-conviction rule applies equally to convictions outside Great Britain: s 1(4); but only if the conduct amounting to the offence would constitute an offence in Great Britain: s 6(6)(c).

3. Excluded sentences

If, at the other extreme, the sentence imposed for the subsequent conviction is one which is *excluded* from rehabilitation (see page 6), then the effect is to exclude not only the second, but also the first, conviction permanently from any possibility of rehabilitation under the Act: s 1(1).

Example

1/1/80 Convicted of theft, fined £100. Rehabilitation period (five years) due to end 31/12/84 if no further conviction of an offence triable on indictment before that date.

1/1/83 Convicted of burglary, sent to prison for three months. Rehabilitation period for the latter offence (seven years) due to end 31/12/89, and the earlier conviction does not now become spent until that date.

1/1/84 Convicted of robbery, sent to prison for three years. This is a sentence excluded from rehabilitation, and none of the convictions will ever become spent.

Because an excluded sentence has no rehabilitation period the curious situation arises that an offender can be worse off by receiving a lesser sentence. For example, if he is fined in 1984 and fined again in 1985 the effect of s 6(4) is to extend the rehabilitation period of the earlier offence to the date of expiry of the later. If, on the other hand, the offender had received an excluded sentence for the earlier offence, it would not have acted to extend the rehabilitation period of the later.
Receiving an excluded sentence *after* a period of rehabilitation has no effect on the spent conviction.

4. Disqualification periods not to count

The only exception to the subsequent-offence rule is that, in assessing the rehabilitation period of the earlier offence, periods arising from orders of disqualification, disability, prohibition or other penalty are disregarded: s 6(5) (a provision criticised, somewhat harshly, by *Current Law Statutes* for its "sheer incomprehensibility"). In such cases the later conviction will only have effect under this provision if it takes place within the rehabilitation period of any other sentence imposed by the earlier offence. In the words of the Minister of State, moving the amendment which resulted in this provision, the effect of s 6(5) is to confine the impeding action of a subsequent sentence on a previous one in the course of becoming spent to the sentence proper and not to any disqualification period which extends it. If, for example, a man is fined, he said, and disqualified from driving for ten years, the rehabilitation period will be ten years, but the delaying effect of any outstanding convictions will, assuming the later offence is indictable, be the five-year period appropriate to the fine. This rule applies not only to road traffic disqualifications, but to disqualifications of all other types, as well as to all disabilities, prohibitions or other penalties.

Example

1/1/80 Convicted of causing death by reckless driving; sentenced to six months' imprisonment (rehabilitation period seven years) and disqualified for life from driving.

6/1/87 Convicted of theft, fined £50 (rehabilitation period five years). This conviction will still become spent notwithstanding that the earlier conviction never can, because it is the disqualification and not the substantive sentence which keeps the earlier conviction "live". Had the second conviction occurred on 6/1/80, the rehabilitation period would have been extended to the end of the seven-year period attracted by the sentence of imprisonment.

This works both ways, that is to say, not only is a rehabilitation period arising from a disqualification not extended by a later conviction but such a period does not itself serve to extend any earlier rehabilitation period.

5. Probation and conditional discharge

If during the currency of a probation order or an order of conditional discharge the offender is convicted of a further offence but not sentenced for the original offence, this has exactly the same effect as a conviction during the rehabilitation period of any other sentence, that is to say, the rehabilitation period of the other original order and that of the subsequent offence both expire at the date of expiry of the later of the two: s 6(4). Provided only that:

(a) the later offence is triable on indictment; and
(b) an excluded sentence is not passed for the later offence.

If in the circumstances the offender is also sentenced for the original offence, this brings into play the further rule in s 6(2) of the 1974 Act, the effect of which, taken together with s 6(4), is that the rehabilitation periods appropriate to

(a) the probation etc order,
(b) the further offence, and
(c) the sentence subsequently imposed for the original offence,

expire at the date of expiry of the one which expires last.

Example:

If an offender is put on probation for two years (rehabilitation period two years) and, shortly afterwards, commits and is convicted of a further offence for which he is sent to prison for a year (rehabilitation period ten years) and is at the same time fined for the original offence (rehabilitation period five years) the rehabilitation period appropriate to all three will be ten years with effect from the date of the second conviction.

In any case the passing of an excluded sentence (see page 6) for a later offence excludes from rehabilitation any unspent probation order or order of conditional discharge.

6. Punishment for breach

An offender who breaks *the terms* of a probation order may, according to s 6 of the Powers of Criminal Courts Act 1973 either:

(a) be sentenced for the original offence (in which

case the rehabilitation period for the original order or the subsequent sentence is extended by virtue of s 6(2) of the 1974 Act to the later of the two expiry dates); or

(b) be punished for the breach by means of a fine, attendance centre order or community service order, the probation order being allowed to continue.

Dealing solely with the situation at (a) above, where the order was made by a magistrates' court, such a punishment would not appear to fall within the further-offence provisions of s 6(4), since the "offence" or breach cannot be tried on indictment: s 6(6)(a). Its effect, therefore, must be as a second or subsequent sentence passed for the original offence which, by virtue of s 6(2), applies to the rehabilitation period of the original conviction the period appropriate to the fine etc, if this would result in it expiring later.

Example

If an offender placed on probation for three years (rehabilitation period three years) is subsequently fined for failing to report to his supervising officer (rehabilitation period five years) the rehabilitation period for the conviction is five years from the date of the sentence for the breach.

Similar principles apply to offenders punished for breach of the terms of a community service order.

The situation sometimes arises where a person who was put on probation or made the subject of an order of conditional discharge has *after becoming rehabilitated* been dealt with in respect of the original offence, for example where a probationer absconds only to be arrested after the end of the probation period. In these circumstances s 6(3) of the 1974 Act provides that the rehabilitation period for the probation order or order of conditional discharge is continued until the period appropriate to the new sentence expires. Effectively, therefore, this extends the rehabilitation period for the original order, so that the offender is deemed not to have become rehabilitated during the intervening period. (It should be noticed that the Act speaks, somewhat confusingly, of "breach of conditional discharge or probation". There is of course no such thing as a breach of a conditional discharge, but it is clear that what is contemplated is the commission of a further offence during the period of conditional discharge. Defiance of the *terms* of a probation order is the usual meaning of the term "breach", but it would appear here as if the legislature were also contemplating the commission of a further offence while on probation.)

Chapter 6

Questions in court

One of the principal objects of the framers of the Act was to protect a rehabilitated person from having to acknowledge the existence of spent convictions in court. The Act seeks to achieve this by *rendering inadmissible in any proceedings before a judicial authority evidence to prove the existence of a spent conviction and by providing that no one in those proceedings may be asked and, if asked, may not be required to answer any question relating to his past which cannot be answered without acknowledging or referring to a spent conviction or its ancillary circumstances:* s 4(1). As will be seen later (page 27) there are a number of important exceptions to this rule.

While this provision does not prevent the rehabilitated person from disclosing a spent conviction, it absolves him from all consequences, including prosecution for perjury, if he should choose to conceal it. This protection applies, not only to the parties in the case and their witnesses, but to any person referred to in evidence.

Ancillary circumstances are widely defined in s 4(5) as including not only the offence or offences the subject of the conviction, but also the conduct constituting the offence, the trial and its preliminaries, as well as anything to do with the sentence and any appeal.

1. The Bar Council's opinion

While these provisions may appear straightforward enough, in practice they can give rise to difficulties. In the course of its opinion of 24 March 1975 the Bar Council expressed the following view so far as civil proceedings were concerned:

> It seems clear, . . . that s 4(1) is intended to prevent the re-hashing of a person's past convictions in any civil proceedings otherwise than as specifically provided for under s 7(2)(f) and 7(3). It follows therefrom that no questions may be asked of a witness, however obliquely, that might tend to establish that he has been the subject of criminal proceedings leading to a spent conviction – although, presumably, no objection could be taken if the proceedings had led to an acquittal.
>
> A more difficult question relates to the duty resting on counsel who appears on behalf of the subject of the spent conviction. Clearly he is not required to disclose such a matter, and indeed, subject only to his client's consent under s 7(2)(f) may not do so; but is he permitted to put questions to his client in such a way as to elicit answers which tend to indicate a previous clean record?
>
> It is said, by the Home Office, that s 4(1) was intended to permit the direct answer "no" to the direct question "have you any previous convictions?", and that the prohibition in s 4(1)(b) was intended to prevent the type of question which indirectly elicits the fact of a spent conviction, eg "on such a date, were you in prison?"
>
> However, the working of s 4 seems to present formidable difficulties in the way of such a construction, and the Council regards it as preferable, at least until a definitive ruling can be given by the Courts, to follow the more obvious interpretation of the section, and recommends that no question whatever should be asked by counsel relating directly or indirectly to a person's previous record, where such record is excluded from consideration by the Act. Any other course would, in the Council's view, offend against the clear duty on counsel never knowingly to mislead the Court, the more so in circumstances where his

opponent is prevented, by the same Act, from correcting the impression so created.

Defamation

Subject to the special provisions set out in s 8 of the Act, it would seem that identical considerations apply to defamation actions as in other civil proceedings.

It may be mentioned that the term "shall not be required to answer" has been held to be inappropriate to examination in chief: *per* Lord Reid in *Jones* v *DPP* (1962) in relation to the Criminal Evidence Act 1898, a statute which bears interesting comparison with the 1974 Act.

2. Arbitrators and tribunals

The protection against disclosure of spent convictions in court applies not only to courts of law, but to proceedings before any judicial authority. This term is widely defined in s 4(6) to include proceedings before arbitrators and tribunals of all kinds. Criminal proceedings and a wide range of civil proceedings are specially exempted (see Chapter 7). In all other proceedings there are two circumstances in which evidence of spent convictions may be admitted and demanded. These are (a) by direction of the court, and (b) with the consent of the rehabilitated person.

3. Admission by direction of the court

In all except the exempted proceedings (see Chapter 7) the court may at any stage dispense with the restrictions concerning questions about spent convictions where it is satisfied in the light of any considerations which appear to be relevant, including any evidence which has been or may be adduced, that justice cannot otherwise be done: s 7(3). "Satisfied" means having made up its mind, not "satisfied beyond reasonable doubt' (cf *Blyth* v *Blyth* (1966)). In such a case the court may admit and require evidence of spent convictions, and may determine any issues to which the evidence relates in disregard, so far as necessary, of the provisions of s 4(1). This means not only that the evidence becomes admissible but that the court may compel disclosure.

By the words "so far as necessary" Parliament would appear to be enjoining the courts to restrict to the very minimum their use of this power to dispense with the Act's protection. No guidelines are set down as to when the interests of justice should override the interests of a rehabilitated person, but the power is clearly intended to be used only to the extent necessary for the purpose in hand. For example, if the interests of justice should demand admission of the fact of a spent conviction, the details of the offence itself and the sentence imposed should not be mentioned unless they too are necessary in order that justice should be done. In the case of *Reynolds* v *Phoenix* (1978) the Court of Appeal declined to direct that evidence of a spent conviction was material and ought to be admitted when the judge at first instance had failed to reach any conclusion on these issues. "This would in my judgement", said Waller LJ, "be a usurpation of the function of the judge who has not himself pronounced on the question. It is his responsibility to deal with it having regard to all the circumstances of the case as presented before him which may affect the justice of the matter between the parties." Wherever the question of exercising this power arises care should be taken according to the nature of the tribunal to reach the decision whether to direct admission or not in such a way that, should it eventually be decided that disclosure is unnecessary, the rehabilitated person's rights would not have been lost by the spent conviction having been mentioned publicly.

4. Admission by consent

Any party or witness to court proceedings may consent to waive the protection of the Act so far as questions in court are concerned: s 7(2)(f). Presumably, it is the duty of the court to ensure that the consent is real in the sense that the rehabilitated person understands the consequence of his act. This could entail the court making an explanation of the law to the witness or to any party who is not legally represented.

In the course of its opinion of 24 March 1975 the Bar Council advised:

> Provision is made under s 7(2)(f) for a person in any proceedings in which he is a party or witness to consent to the admission of evidence relating to previous convictions. This is clearly a consent that can only be given personally and counsel would be under a duty to take specific instructions before consenting on his client's behalf.

It should be noticed that there is no provision by which persons who are not parties or witnesses may consent to admission of evidence about their spent convictions, and the only way in which they may be referred to in other than exempted proceedings (see Chapter 7) is by a direction of the court under s 7(3).

Chapter 7

Exempt proceedings

There is a wide range of judicial proceedings in which the protection afforded by the Act to a rehabilitated person does not apply. They are proceedings relating to:

- adoption;
- guardianship;
- wardship;
- marriage;
- custody;
- care or control of or access to any minor;
- the provision by any person of accommodation, care or schooling for minors;
- care proceedings;
- variation and discharge of care and supervision orders;
- criminal proceedings; and
- service disciplinary proceedings.

In all these cases the Act imposes no restrictions on the admission in evidence of spent convictions or the circumstances surrounding them: s 7(2).

It may sometimes be difficult to define just when proceedings "relate to" any of the listed matters. For example, in the course of matrimonial proceedings in the magistrates' courts the issue of custody can be determined without the restrictions on admitting spent convictions, but not the question of whether a matrimonial offence has taken place, although in practice evidence on the two matters may often be heard at the same time. In such a case it is the duty of the court totally to disregard spent convictions when it comes to determining the matrimonial issue.

The criminal courts are required, as a matter of practice rather than statute, to reduce the disclosure of spent convictions to a minimum. See Chapter 8.

Chapter 8

In the criminal courts

Section 7(2) of the Act excludes from its scope *the determination of any issue and the admission or requirement of any evidence relating to spent convictions or their ancillary circumstances in any criminal proceedings before a court in Great Britain.*

There seems little doubt that this provision applies to the citation of spent convictions after a plea of guilty or a finding of guilt, despite the fact that the normal practice is for an offender's record to be read out or put in writing otherwise than on oath. The point is that if a conviction is challenged it must be proved by sworn evidence or by any of the statutory methods of proof, and as such falls within the terms of s 7(2).

But previous convictions may be admissible even during the course of a criminal trial, for example, in accordance with the Criminal Evidence Act 1898, to attack the credibility of a witness or even the accused. Commenting on the effects of s 7(2) on these rules the Bar Council, in the course of its opinion of 24 March 1975, observed:

> Section 4(1) requires that in all judicial proceedings the rehabilitated person "shall be treated for all purposes in law" as a person of good character. No evidence is admissible in "any proceedings before a judicial authority" to prove the spent convictions, and no questions may be asked in respect of them.
>
> Section 7(2)(a) then excludes the effect of s 4(1) in respect of criminal proceedings. The wording is very curious. It reads: "Nothing in section 4(1) above shall affect the determination of any issue or prevent the admission or requirement of any evidence relating to a

person's previous convictions or to circumstances ancillary thereto in any criminal proceedings . . . " Doubts as to whether this has only a limited application would appear to be removed by s 7(3) which refers to s 7(2) and by which it says "Section 4(1) has no application". It seems therefore by this somewhat tortuous route the Act has no effect in the criminal courts.

The Attorney-General agrees with the foregoing conclusions.

1. The Practice Direction

Nevertheless, the Lord Chief Justice wishes the spirit of the Act to be complied with even in the criminal courts so far as is compatible with the interests of justice. The practice in the Crown Court is governed by the following Direction:

1. The effect of s 4(1) of the Rehabilitation of Offenders Act, 1974, is that a person who has become a rehabilitated person for the purpose of the Act in respect of a conviction (known as a "spent" conviction) shall be treated for all purposes in law as a person who has not committed or been charged with or prosecuted for or convicted of or sentenced for the offence or offences which were the subject of that conviction.
2. Section 4(1) of the 1974 Act does not apply to evidence given in any criminal proceedings (s 7(2)(a)). Convictions are often disclosed in such proceedings. When the Bill was before the House of Commons on the 28th June, 1974, the hope was expressed that the Lord Chief Justice would issue a Practice Direction for the guidance of the Crown Courts with a view to reducing disclosure of spent convictions to a minimum and securing uniformity of approach.
3. During the trial of a criminal charge reference to previous convictions (and therefore to spent

convictions) can arise in a number of ways. The most common is when the character of the accused or a witness is sought to be attacked by reference to his criminal record; but there are, of course, cases where previous convictions are relevant and admissible as, for instance, to prove system.

4. It is not possible to give general directions which will govern all these different situations, but it is recommended that both Court and Counsel should give effect to the general intention of Parliament by never referring to a spent conviction when such reference can be reasonably avoided. If unnecessary references to spent convictions are eliminated much will have been achieved.

5. After a verdict of guilty the Court must be provided with a statement of the Defendant's record for the purposes of sentence. The record supplied should contain all previous convictions, but those which are spent should, so far as practicable, be marked as such.

6. No one should refer in Open Court to a spent conviction without the authority of the Judge, which authority should not be given unless the interests of justice so require.

7. When passing sentence the Judge should make no reference to a spent conviction unless it is necessary to do so for the purpose of explaining the sentence to be passed.

(Practice Direction [1975] 2 All ER 1072)

The direction was referred to in the case of *R* v *Paraskeva* (1982) where a conviction was quashed when the prosecution failed to inform the defence of the fact that the complainant to a charge of assault occasioning actual bodily harm had a spent conviction for theft. Where the appellant was a man of good character, it was said, the judge at first instance would not have refused his consent, if asked, for the complainant's conviction to be put to the witness.

2. Proceedings in magistrates' courts

While the Practice Direction does not apply in terms to the magistrates' courts the implications of the Act have been considered by the Home Secretary in consultation with the Magistrates' Association, the Justices' Clerks' Society, the Chief Metropolitan Magistrate, and the Association of Chief Police Officers. The Secretary of State considers that magistrates' courts will wish to follow, so far as possible, the practice commended below, which reflects the tenor of the Lord Chief Justice's Practice Direction. What this implies, broadly speaking, is that when evidence of antecedents is given following conviction, no oral reference should be made to any spent conviction unless it has influenced the court in determining sentence. In the course of Home Office circular no. 98/1975, dated 24 June 1975, the following views were expressed:

> The Home Secretary hopes that magistrates' courts will continue, so far as practicable, to follow the guidance on the citing of previous convictions set out in the Home Office circular no. 17/1973. In addition, to avoid unnecessary references to and publication of spent convictions, the following practice is commended:
>
> (i) In all cases where it is practicable, a typed list of all the defendant's previous convictions should be submitted to the court by the police. Spent convictions should be included, and the police officer submitting the list should normally attempt to indicate on the list which these are.
>
> (ii) Where it is not possible because of lack of time to produce a typed list, the list should be presented in manuscript. Courts and/or police authorities may consider it appropriate to produce a simple *pro forma* for this purpose,
>
> (iii) Even when it is necessary to submit details of previous convictions in manuscript, the list should include all the defendant's previous convictions, including spent convictions, so marked so far as possible.

(iv) It may not always be practicable particularly in the busier courts to produce full details of previous convictions, and in such cases the prosecution should not be required to provide any more information than they are at present. The practice adopted at present in some courts in such cases, where full details of only the last three convictions are cited, with a brief summary of other convictions where relevant, should continue to be used when this cannot be avoided. Cases where such convictions may be relevant include those where a juvenile or young adult has had a previous custodial sentence, which may be particularly relevant to whether, for example, a detention centre order would be an appropriate disposal for the current offence.

(v) Although the prosecuting officer or solicitor should indicate on the written list which convictions, if any, appear to be spent, it will be for the court to decide, on the advice of the clerk if necessary, whether a conviction is spent and whether it should be taken into account in determining sentence.

(vi) Oral evidence as to previous convictions should not necessarily be completely excluded, particularly when the only alternative would be to request a remand. Oral evidence should, however, be given only with the consent, or at the express direction, of the court. If oral evidence is given, care should be taken wherever possible to avoid any reference to specific convictions, which could include some which are spent.

(vii) Courts will no doubt wish to take spent convictions into account in determining sentence only when they are satisfied that it is essential in the interests of justice to do so. In cases where the court proposes to take spent convictions into account, and where they are to be cited orally as a result, the defendant or his counsel should be given the opportunity to refer to them in

> mitigation of sentence. In the light of the Parliamentary proceedings which led to the enactment of the Rehabilitation of Offenders Act 1974 and of the previous guidance concerning the citing in court of old and irrelevant spent convictions on the occasion of sentence, the Secretary of State believes that magistrates' courts may wish to give their reasons when deciding to take account of spent convictions, and to admit oral testimony of them.

The guidance in Home Office circular no. 98/1975 dealt only with reference to spent convictions in the context of consideration of a defendant's previous convictions for the purpose of determining sentence. The Practice Direction also seeks to discourage unnecessary references to spent convictions at other stages of criminal proceedings where previous convictions may be admissible in evidence. Home Office Circular no. 130/1975, dated 6 August 1975, expresses the view that magistrates' courts will no doubt wish to follow the Crown Court in responding to the guidance from the Lord Chief Justice that spent convictions should be referred to in open court only when such references cannot in the interests of justice reasonably be avoided.

3. Non-convictions not to be cited

A small change in the general law affecting the citing of previous convictions in criminal courts after conviction is contained in s 7(5). This *prohibits the inclusion in any list of previous convictions of any order made by a court otherwise than on a conviction.*

In fact, this is no more than a declaration of what should formerly have happened, but a practice had grown up of including in these documents a variety of matters which could never be described as previous convictions. The effect of this provision is that the offender's record produced to the court may not contain, for example, a bind-over on a "peeping tom" arrested for breach of the peace. (Where an offender is bound over as part of his sentence for an offence there is no objection to this fact appearing on the record.) Needless to say, acquittals and convictions reversed on appeal should never appear on the record produced to the court.

Probation orders and orders of conditional and absolute discharge are specifically exempt from this rule despite the Powers of Criminal Courts Act 1973, s 13(1), as are care proceedings alleging the offence condition: s 1(4). However, care proceedings, whether arising from the offence condition or not, should never be listed as previous convictions for the simple reason that they cannot result in a conviction.

There is nothing to prevent non-convictions, such as care proceedings or bind-overs, from being mentioned, where relevant, by the police or probation officer as part of the offender's antecedent history, so long as they are not included among the list of previous convictions.

Chapter 9

Protection out of court

The Act is not concerned only with questions in court: it also aims to protect the rehabilitated person from the obligation to disclose spent convictions out of court and, more optimistically perhaps, from certain forms of prejudice to which he might otherwise be liable, in all except a number of excepted occupations and cases.

1. Protection from the need to disclose

Subject to the excepted cases, *a rehabilitated person may answer questions about his past as if they did not relate to his spent convictions:* s 4(2)(a). For example, when answering questions from an employer or prospective employer, a trade union or an insurance company, even those which ask specifically about his previous convictions, the rehabilitated person may frame his answer in a way which either ignores or even actually denies the existence of his spent convictions.

If the protection of the Act were confined to spent *convictions* it would be an easy matter for questions to be phrased so as to evade it, but it extends to circumstances ancillary to the conviction, a phrase which is defined very widely in s 4(5).

There is nothing in the Act which prevents anyone from disclosing his spent convictions; it merely provides that anyone who chooses to hide them shall be treated in law as if he had told the truth. The Act gives the same protection to anyone else answering a question about a rehabilitated person, although once again there is nothing to stop him telling the whole truth if he thinks fit.

2. Protection from the consequences of non-disclosure

Subject to the excepted cases, *if a rehabilitated person fails to disclose a spent conviction in response to a question about his past he may not be subjected to any liability or otherwise prejudiced in law for doing so: s 4(2)(b).*

Some contracts are governed by the principle of *uberrimae fidei* (the utmost good faith) which requires a proposal for insurance, for example, to contain all relevant information *whether asked for or not.* In a proposal for fidelity insurance, say, the existence of a prior conviction for dishonesty could very well be relevant but for the terms of the Act, and non-disclosure could render voidable any policy which might subsequently issue. To give protection against this and related obligations the Act provides that *legal obligation to disclose shall not extend to spent convictions, whether of the person questioned or anyone else:* s 4(3)(a). This can lead to some strange consequences. As the commentary to *Halsbury's Statutes* points out, a proposer for a motor insurance policy is bound to disclose an accident which led to no criminal proceedings, but may conceal one which led to his conviction and disqualification. (For an example of a case in which s 4 was pleaded in relation to an insurance policy see *Arif v Excess Insurance Group Ltd* (1982)).

3. Protection in employment

Perhaps one of the most important areas of protection afforded by the Act concerns the field of employment. Even with all these precautions it could still come about that an employer or other person in authority could get to know of a spent conviction and regard it, rightly or wrongly, as reason for believing a person whom the law regards as rehabilitated to be no longer suitable for his employment. The Act accordingly provides that, subject to the excepted cases, *spent convictions or a failure to disclose them are not a proper ground for dismissing or excluding anyone from his employment or from any office, profession or occupation, or otherwise prejudicing him in his occupation or employment:* s 4(3)(b).

The effect of this it to make it unlawful to dismiss an employee solely because of the existence of a spent conviction *no matter how relevant that may be.* It would, for example, prevent a trade union from excluding a member by reason of a spent conviction. (Compare the former position in *Faramus v Film Artistes Association* (1964).) Admission to and exclusion from certain professions is excluded from the scope of the Act by virtue of ministerial Order – See Chapter 10. Dismissal or exclusion is not a criminal offence, but the rehabilitated person would be able to enforce his rights through the civil courts or by recourse to an industrial tribunal in the same way as someone wrongfully dismissed for any other cause. On the other hand, there has hitherto been no right to be engaged in employment because the law has recognized no bounds to the right of an employer to engage whom he likes. Nor does the Act provide any machinery whereby the novel right not to be refused employment on account of spent convictions may be enforced. No doubt, the courts will not be slow to adapt existing remedies.

4. References

Since the protection against disclosure of spent convictions extends not only to the rehabilitated person, but to anyone else answering questions about him, an employer or friend may give a reference for a rehabilitated person which ignores or even denies the existence of his spent convictions: s 4(2). He would incur no liability for doing so even if there were a contractual or other legal duty to make full disclosure: s 4(3).

On the other hand there is nothing to compel a referee to conceal spent convictions and, as will be seen later (Chapter 11), he will not be liable in damages for revealing these unless it can be proved that he did so out of malice.

The Secretary of State has by order exempted from these provisions a number of occupations and cases, which are described in Chapter 10.

5. Going abroad

It is important to remember that the Act applies to Great Britain only, it has no effect so far as the laws of other countries are concerned, so that applicants for immigration and work permits and for travel visas to the USA still have to make full disclosure of their criminal record or, in the words of the *Justice* report, risk the consequences. Some foreign countries have legislation similar to the Rehabilitation of Offenders Act, but to discover what safeguards apply it is necessary to consult the laws of the country concerned.

Chapter 10

Excepted cases

Many have seen it as a weakness of the Act that there have to be so many exceptions to its provisions. The effect of a ministerial Order is to qualify the effects of legal rehabilitation substantially when it comes to matters of national security, the care of the young, the administration of justice and certain other cases where Parliament clearly does not trust the effect of its own legislation. However that may be, out-of-court protection of the Act cannot properly be grasped without recognition of the many occupations and cases from which it is specifically excluded. Provided that the person questioned is given any necessary warning as to his lack of rights, his situation so far as the excepted employment or activity is concerned is exactly as if the Act had not been passed.

1. Excepted occupations

The Secretary of State, acting under his powers in s 7(4) of the Act and with the prior approval of Parliament, has by Order (the Rehabilitation of Offenders Act 1974 (Exceptions) Order 1975, SI 1975 No 1022, the text of which is contained in Appendix 2) excluded a number of professions, occupations and offices from the effects of subss (1) and (2). The effect of this, broadly speaking, is that a person may be questioned about his spent convictions in order to assess his suitability for specified offices or occupations or for admission to specified professions. Furthermore, a spent conviction may be relied upon as a ground for dismissal of such persons from office or employment, or for dismissal or exclusion from their profession. This applies not only to the legal, medical, accountancy and teaching professions, but also to a wide range of jobs involving access to minors and others in vulnerable situations, as well as to police, judges, probation officers and others concerned with the administration of justice. The existence of a spent conviction or a failure to disclose it in these cases could result in dismissal or other harmful consequences without benefit of the protection otherwise afforded by the Act. Where minors are concerned the exception may in certain circumstances extend even to persons living in the same household as the person questioned. (See article 3(aa) of the 1975 Order in Appendix 2).

2. Certificates and licences

The same Order allows questions to be asked concerning spent convictions in relation to applications for certain certificates and licences, for example concerning firearms, explosives and gaming, and for such convictions to be taken into account by the appropriate authorities.

Failure to disclose a spent conviction could result in the refusal or loss of the licence, certificate etc, or even in prosecution for non-disclosure.

In all these cases the Order stipulates that the normal rules regarding rehabilitation shall only be lifted where the person questioned is informed at the time the question is asked that, by virtue of the Order, spent convictions are to be disclosed.

3. National security

The Order allows details of spent convictions to be demanded and taken into account by or on behalf of the Crown and certain public bodies when assessing for the purpose of safeguarding national security suitability for office or employment. Here again, the exclusion only applies if the person questioned is informed at the time that, by virtue of the Order, spent convictions must be disclosed *for the purpose of safeguarding national security.*

4. Financial regulation

The Financial Services Act 1986 restricts the provision of financial services to members of self-regulatory organisations and recognised professional bodies, and to persons directly authorised by the Securities and Investments Board. In order to assist in that regulation s 189 of the Financial Services Act removes the protection of s 4(1) of the 1974 Act from certain proceedings provided that the spent conviction is for:

(a) an offence involving fraud or other dishonesty; or

(b) an offence under legislation relating to companies (including insider dealing), building societies, industrial and provident societies, credit unions, friendly societies, insurance, banking or other financial services, insolvency, consumer credit or consumer protection.

The proceedings concerned are those relating to the exclusion or expulsion of a member of a recognised professional body or a self-regulatory organisation, and other proceedings listed in Sch 14 to the Act.

The same provision removes from the protection of the 1974 Act questions about such spent convictions put out of court, provided that:

(a) the question is put by or on behalf of certain persons and relates to specified individuals (whether or not the person is questioned); and

(b) the person questioned is informed when the question is put that, by virtue of s 189, convictions for any offence are to be disclosed. The persons concerned include the Securities and Investments Board, self-regulatory organisations and recognised professional bodies.

Finally, s 189 removes from specified persons the protection against loss of office, occupation etc provided by the 1974 Act in respect of the spent convictions mentioned in the section.

For the text of s 189 of the Financial Services Act 1986 see Appendix 3. A broadly similar provision is contained in s 95 of the Banking Act 1987 concerning the persons regulated under that measure. For the text of that section see Appendix 4.

Further exceptions to s 4 of the 1974 Act are made by the Rehabilitation of Offenders Act 1974 (Exceptions) Order 1975 (Appendix 2). Firstly, it provides that subs (2) shall not apply in specified circumstances to questions relating to certain offences (referred to in the Order as "relevant offences") put by or on behalf of the Building Societies Commission ("the Commission") or building societies. Secondly, it provides that subs (3)(b) shall not apply to certain specified actions taken by the Commission in relation to building societies or to the dismissal or exclusion by a building society of a person from his office by reason of a spent conviction for a relevant offence. Thirdly, if provides that s 4(1) shall not apply to certain specified proceedings before the Commission or to any proceedings by way of appeal against, or review of, any decision taken by the Commission to the extent that those proceedings raise issues relating to a spent conviction for a relevant offence.

Chapter 11

Defamation

Since a rehabilitated person is treated for all purposes in law as not having committed or been charged with or prosecuted for or convicted of or sentenced for an offence it follows that to say otherwise would in law be an untruth. To publish an untruthful statement which tends to lower a person in the estimation of right-thinking members of society generally or which tends to make them shun or avoid him may amount to the tort of defamation. A reference to a spent conviction in a newspaper article, for example, could thus give ground for a claim for damages notwithstanding that in fact, as opposed to law, the reference was correct. It was this possibility which gave rise to the comment in the interim report of the *Faulks Committee on Defamation* that "the bill, if published in anything like its present form, would be a serious and unjustified inroad on the freedom of the individual to tell the truth". Fortunately for truth, the bill underwent various changes in its passage though Parliament which, while not disturbing its basic proposition, nevertheless altered its practical consequences considerably.

1. The defence of justification

Foremost among these changes was the last-minute retention of the defence of justification, that is the defence that a statement which is the subject of an action of defamation is true: s 8(3). It would be foolish to deny that retention of this defence has deprived the Act of much of its force so far as press and similar comment is concerned, but as least it avoids the objectionable situation where a truthful statement made in good faith could have given rise to a risk of damages. In this very important way, therefore, the defence of justification preserves the right of the public to be made aware of matters of genuine public interest.

To avoid the spiteful resurrection of spent convictions, however, the Act provides that a defence of justification may be rebutted where the plaintiff can prove that the statement was published with malice: s 8(5). The term "malice" is not further defined in the Act, but presumably means an abuse of the right to speak the truth by spiteful or wrongful or improper motive on the part of the defendant: cf *Winfield on Tort,* 6th edn, p 300. In *Herbage* v *Pressdram* (1985) Griffiths LJ, giving the judgment, said that he took the word in this subsection to mean published with some irrelevant, spiteful or improper motive.

That case concerned an application for an injunction to restrain the defendants from further publication of the plaintiff's spent convictions. Griffiths LJ said that:

> The rehabilitated person, for the purposes of the law of libel, is placed at a real advantage by virtue of the fact that he has kept clear of crime for the requisite period. It seems to me that this very closely equates the position with the case where a defendant relies on a defence of qualified privilege. In such a case, the law is now well settled. Only if, at the interlocutory stage, the evidence of malice is absolutely overwhelming will the court intervene to restrain publication by way of interlocutory injunction: see *William Coulson & Sons* v *James Coulson & Co* (1887); TLR 846.

Where an alleged defamatory statement refers to an offence which is the subject of a conviction, s 13 of the Civil Evidence Act 1968 continues to permit the defendant to rely on the conviction as *prima facie* evidence of the offence.

But justification is not the only defence retained by the Act for those accused of defamation of rehabilitated persons. The defendant to such an action may also plead the defences of fair comment and absolute or qualified privilege:

s 8(3). Both these defences are available whether the statement complained of was true or not.

2. Fair comment

The defence of fair comment consists of an assertion that publication of the statement complained of was a fair comment on a matter of public interest. It has been said, for example, that "whoever fills a public position renders himself open to public discussion and if any part of his public acts is wrong he must accept the attack as a necessary though unpleasant circumstance attaching to his position": per Bramwell B in *Kelly* v *Sherlock* (1866). Under the general law of defamation malice is sufficient to rebut a defence of a fair comment.

Since the defence of fair comment is restricted to matters of opinion rather than matters of fact it is frequently pleaded along with the defence of justification in what is called the "rolled-up" plea. Nothing in the Act prevents such a plea in a case of this nature although, as has already been said, proof of malice on the part of the defendant is sufficient to defeat both limbs of this plea.

3. The defence of privilege

The reporting of certain events and the making of statements in certain circumstances are said to enjoy privilege, either absolute or qualified, against actions of defamation because they are cases where the public interest in freedom of speech outweighs the rights of the defamed persons. The defence of privilege is specifically retained by s 8(3) of the Act. Wherever possible, the defendant will wish to plead that the statement was made in privileged circumstances, because this may afford a defence even where he is unable to prove the truth of the statement. The difference between absolute and qualified privilege is that qualified privilege is no defence where the plaintiff can prove that the statement was actuated by malice.

Examples are:

Absolute Privilege

- statements made in Parliament and in Parliamentary papers;
- relevant statements made in the course of judicial proceedings;
- fair and accurate newspaper and broadcast reports of judicial proceedings;
- communications between solicitor and client;
- communications between one officer of state and another.

Qualified Privilege

- fair and accurate reports of Parliamentary proceedings;
- fair and accurate reports of judicial proceedings to which the public are admitted;
- statements made between people with common interests;
- statements made by persons having a duty to communicate to persons having any interests to receive (for example, one employer writing to another about a reference for a job);
- fair and accurate reports of the proceedings of any public meeting in the United Kingdom and of certain bodies.

A defendant pleading qualified privilege may rely on a spent conviction when seeking to rebut an allegation of malice: s 8(4).

4. Reports of judicial proceedings

Where the defence to an action of defamation arising from a spent conviction is that the matter complained of constituted a fair and accurate report of judicial proceedings the defendant may not rely on evidence relating to spent convictions if the alleged defamatory statement contained material which had been held in those proceedings to be inadmissible under s 4(1) of the Act: s 8(6). It should be noted that this provision refers to evidence "ruled to be inadmissible". Presumably, if the question of admissibility had not been raised and ruled upon in the course of the proceedings it could not be said to have been *ruled* inadmissible, since this implies a ruling of the court rather than of the statute; in which case the defendant would still be able to rely on the defence of qualified privilege, however inadmissible the evidence might have been under the Act.

Bona fide series of law reports and reports or accounts in lectures or for other educational purposes are given special protection by being made exempt from this rule. A defence of qualified privilege may thus be maintained even where the report complained of contained evidence ruled to be inadmissible under the Act: s 8(7).

Chapter 12

Unauthorised disclosure

Nothing in the Act prohibits or restricts the keeping by the police or anyone else of records of previous convictions, but it is concerned to see that details of spent convictions should not get into the wrong hands. For this purpose the protection afforded by the law of defamation is more apparent than real, particularly in the light of the defences already described. In an attempt to restrict disclosure at source the Act makes it an offence for *anyone who in the course of his official duties has or has had custody of or access to official records or the information contained therein to disclose specified information obtained in the course of those duties, but only if he knows or has reasonable cause to suspect that it is specified information and only if the disclosure was made otherwise than in the course of official duties:* s 9(2).

"Specified information" means information imputing that an identifiable living person has committed, been charged with, prosecuted for, convicted of or sentenced for an offence which is the subject of a spent conviction: s 9(1). It would therefore be an offence for a police officer to disclose in the course of gossip not merely that someone had been convicted of an offence which is the subject of a spent conviction, but even to say that he had committed the offence or had been accused of it or had received a sentence for it. On the other hand it would not be an offence for an official archivist to disclose John Bunyan's conviction for vagrancy, because the Bedford tinker is no longer a living person. Strangely enough, it is no offence to disclose conduct or proceedings which resulted in an acquittal.

The term "official record" includes police and court records, and records relating to convictions kept by local and public authorities and the armed forces: s 9(1). It does not extend to records kept by companies or private concerns.

It should be noted that it is no offence for anyone with access to official records to disclose specified information which he has read in the newspaper, heard over the garden fence or obtained otherwise than in the course of his official duties.

1. Official duties

The communication of specified information in performance of a statutory or other legal duty seemingly can never be an offence, but the reference to "official duties", although not further defined in the Act, cannot be confined to occasions where the official acts under such a duty. Whitford J had to deal with this question in the case of *X* v *Metropolitan Police Commissioner* (1985). In that case a police officer at the London branch of Interpol had disclosed to the Paris Office details of the plaintiff's spent convictions. The learned judge asked himself what was the mischief to which s 9 was directed? In his view, he said, it is concerned with situations in which persons, who quite rightly become aware of specified information in the course of their official duties, for some reason or another, and in no sense in any way in connection with any duty arising out of their station or office, communicate to some third party that specified information. The police in this country had for many years accepted obligations relating to the transmission of information following requests received. International crime has assumed a significance which, so far as this country is concerned, makes its suppression as important to the inhabitants of this country as the suppression of domestic crime. The plaintiff was denied the declaration he sought.

A police officer, a probation officer or a court official would, seemingly, not commit an offence by disclosing spent convictions in the ordinary course of his work to persons who clearly have a lawful or proper use for them, for purposes connected with:

- the detection of crime
- ordinary court, police and welfare practice and procedures;
- assessing the suitability of a person to have care of the young;
- informing a head teacher of the appearance in court of one of his pupils; and
- the assistance of other officials, for example, communications between one court and another, or between a probation officer and the social services department of a local authority.

Probation officers are often involved in assisting probationers to get jobs. Sometimes they take the view that it is in the interests both of the employer and the probationer that the former should be aware of the probationer's past record. Since this involves a social work decision concerning the probation officer's statutory duty there would seem to be no question of a risk of prosecution under the Act. As to their liability for an action for damages see page 41.

Not everyone with access to official records is liable to prosecution under this section, but only those who have such access in the course of their official duties. An academic statistician given research facilities among police records would commit no offence under the Act by disclosing a spent conviction culled from this source, but a Government statistician might.

A justices' clerk is, by statute, keeper of the register of his magistrates' court and as such has, it is suggested, authority to disclose its contents on his own initiative for any lawful and proper purpose. If in doubt about the propriety of a particular disclosure he has the additional remedy of seeking authorization under r 66(12) of the Magistrates' Courts Rules 1981 which reads:

> Every register shall be open to inspection during reasonable hours by any justice of the peace, or any person authorized in that behalf by a justice of the peace or the Secretary of State.

Further advice to officials is given in Part III of Home Office circular no. 98/1975, dated 24 June 1975.

2. Defences

It is a defence to a charge under s 9(2) for the defendant to prove that disclosure was made:

(a) to the rehabilitated person or to any other person at his request;

(b) to a person reasonably believed to be the rehabilitated person; or

(c) to another at the request of a person reasonably believed to be the rehabilitated person

(s 9(3)).

The offence under s 9(2) is punishable by a fine not exceeding level 4 on the standard scale. Prosecution, however, may only be instituted by or on behalf of the Director of Public Prosecutions: s 9(8).

3. Corrupt practices

The Act also creates a second and more serious offence of *obtaining information from official records by means of fraud, dishonesty or bribe* (s 9(4)), which, by virtue of s 9(7) is punishable by six months' imprisonment and a fine not exceeding level 5 on the standard scale. There is no restriction corresponding to s 9(8).

4. Other offences

It should be remembered that it is an offence under the Official Secrets Act 1911 for anyone in possession or control of information entrusted to him in confidence by a Crown servant (including a police officer) or obtained by him as a Crown servant to communicate that information to an unauthorized person or a person to whom he had no duty to disclose it, or to fail to take reasonable care of the information.

Appendix 1

The Rehabilitation of Offenders Act 1974

An Act to rehabilitate offenders who have not been reconvicted of any serious offence for periods of years, to penalise the unauthorised disclosure of their previous convictions, to amend the law of defamation, and for purposes connected therewith [31 July 1974]

1. Rehabilitated persons and spent convictions

(As amended by the Criminal Law Act 1977, s 47, Sch 9.)

(1) Subject to subsection (2) below, where an individual has been convicted, whether before or after the commencement of this Act, of any offence or offences, and the following conditions are satisfied, that is to say –

(a) he did not have imposed on him in respect of that conviction a sentence which is excluded from rehabilitation under this Act; and

(b) he has not had imposed on him in respect of a subsequent conviction during the rehabilitation period applicable to the first-mentioned conviction in accordance with section 6 below a sentence which is excluded from rehabilitation under this Act;

then, after the end of the rehabilitation period so applicable (including, where appropriate, any extension under section 6(4) below of the period originally applicable to the first-mentioned conviction) or, where that rehabilitation period ended before the commencement of this Act, after the commencement of this Act, that individual shall for the purposes of this Act be treated as a rehabilitated person in respect of the first-mentioned conviction and that conviction shall for those purposes be treated as spent.

(2) A person shall not become a rehabilitated person for the purposes of this Act in respect of a conviction unless he has served or otherwise undergone or complied with any sentence imposed on him in respect of that conviction; but the following shall not, by virtue of this subsection, prevent a person from becoming a rehabilitated person for those purposes –

(a) failure to pay a fine or other sum adjudged to be paid by or imposed on a conviction, or breach of a condition of a recognisance or of a bond of caution to keep the peace or be of good behaviour;

(b) breach of any condition or requirement applicable in relation to a sentence which renders the person to whom it applies liable to be dealt with for the offence for which the sentence was imposed, or, where the sentence was a suspended sentence of imprisonment, liable to be dealt with in respect of that sentence (whether or not, in any case, he is in fact so dealt with);

(c) failure to comply with any requirement of a suspended sentence supervision order.

(2A) Where in respect of a conviction a person has been sentenced to imprisonment with an order under section 47(1) of the Criminal Law Act 1977, he is to be treated for the purposes of subsection (2) above as having served the sentence as soon as he completes service of so much of the sentence as was by that order required to be served in prison.

(3) In this Act "sentence" includes any order made by a court in dealing with a person in respect of his conviction of any offence or offences, other than –

(a) an order for committal or any other order made in default of payment of any fine or other sum adjudged to be paid by or imposed on a conviction, or for want of sufficient distress to satisfy any such fine or other sum;

(b) an order dealing with a person in respect of a suspended sentence of imprisonment.

(4) In this Act, references to a conviction, however expressed, include references –

(a) to a conviction by or before a court outside Great Britain; and

(b) to any finding (other than a finding linked with a finding of insanity) in any criminal proceedings or in care proceedings under section 1 of the Children and Young Persons Act 1969 that a person has committed an offence or done the act or made the omission charged;

and notwithstanding anything in section 9 of the Criminal Justice (Scotland) Act 1949 or section 13 of the Powers of Criminal Courts Act 1973 (conviction of a person put on probation or discharged to be deemed not to be a conviction) a conviction in respect of which an order is made placing the person convicted on probation or discharging him absolutely or conditionally shall be treated as a conviction for the purposes of this Act and the person in question may become a rehabilitated person in respect of that conviction and the conviction a spent conviction for those purposes accordingly.

[**Commentary**]

The commencement of this Act: 1 July 1975: s 11(2).
Sentence: see also s 2.
Excluded from rehabilitation: see s 5(1).

2. Rehabilitation of persons dealt with in service disciplinary proceedings

(As amended by the Armed Forces Act 1976, s 22(5), Sch 9; the Armed Forces Act 1981, s 28(1), Sch 4.)

(1) Subject to the following provisions of this section, for the purposes of this Act any finding that a person is guilty of an offence in respect of any act or omission which was the subject of service disciplinary proceedings shall be treated as a conviction and any punishment awarded or order made by virtue of Schedule 5A to the Army Act 1955 or the Air Force Act 1955 or Schedule 4A to the Naval

Discipline Act 1957 in respect of any such finding shall be treated as a sentence.

(2) Subsection (1) above applies subject to section 17 of the Armed Forces Act 1976 (rehabilitation of civilians), only where either or both of the following conditions is satisfied, that is to say –

(a) the offence in question is an offence to which this subsection applies; or

(b) the punishment awarded is a punishment to which this subsection applies.

(3) Subsection (2) above applies to any offence consisting in the commission of a civil offence and to any offence under, and any offence of attempting to commit an offence under, any of the following enactments, or any corresponding enactment previously in force –

(a) sections 30, 45, 46, 61, 62, 64 and 66 of the Army Act 1955 and the Air Force Act 1955; and

(b) sections 5, 30, 31, 34A, 35, 36 and 37 of the Naval Discipline Act 1957.

(4) Subsection (2) above applies to the following punishments –

(a) imprisonment;

(b) cashiering, discharge with ignominy or dismissal with disgrace from Her Majesty's service;

(c) dismissal from Her Majesty's service;

(d) detention for a term of three months or more; and

(e) detention by virtue of a custodial order made under section 71AA of or Schedule 5A to the Army Act 1955 or the Air Force Act 1955 or under section 43AA of or Schdule 4A to the Naval Discipline Act 1957.

(5) In this Act "service disciplinary proceedings" means any of the following –

(a) any proceedings under the Army Act 1955, the Air Force Act 1955, or the Naval Discipline Act 1957 (whether before a court-martial or before any other court or person authorised thereunder to award a punishment in respect of any offence);

(b) any proceedings under any Act previously in force corresponding to any of the Acts mentioned in paragraph (a) above;

(bb) any proceedings before a Standing Civilian Court established under the Armed Forces Act 1976;

(c) any proceedings under any corresponding enactment or law applying to a force, other than a home force, to which section 4 of the Visiting Forces (British Commonwealth) Act 1933 applies or applied at the time of the proceedings, being proceedings in respect of a member of a home force who is or was at that time attached to the first-mentioned force under that section;

whether in any event those proceedings take place in Great Britain or elsewhere.

[**Commentary**]

Sentence: partially defined in s 1(3).
Home force: see the Visiting Forces (British Commonwealth) Act, s 8(1).

3. Special provision with respect to certain disposals by children's hearings under the Social Work (Scotland) Act 1968

Where a ground for the referral of a child's case to a children's hearing under the Social Work (Scotland) Act 1968 is that mentioned in section 32(2)(g) of that Act (commission by the child of an offence) and that ground has either been accepted by the child and, where necessary, by his parent or been established to the satisfaction of the sheriff under section 42 of that Act, the acceptance or establishment of that ground shall be treated for the purposes of this Act (but not otherwise) as a conviction, and any disposal of the case thereafter by a children's hearing shall be treated for those purposes as a sentence; and references in this Act to a person's being charged with or prosecuted for an offence shall be construed accordingly.

4. Effect of rehabilitation

(1) Subject to sections 7 and 8 below, a person who has become a rehabilitated person for the purposes of this Act in respect of a conviction shall be treated for all purposes in law as a person who has not committed or been charged with or prosecuted of or convicted of or sentenced for the offence or offences which were the subject of that conviction; and, notwithstanding the provisions of any other enactment or rule of law to the contrary, but subject as aforesaid –

(a) no evidence shall be admissible in any proceedings before a judicial authority exercising its jurisdiction or functions in Great Britain to prove that any such person has committed or been charged with or prosecuted for or convicted of or sentenced for any offence which was the subject of a spent conviction; and

(b) a person shall not, in any such proceedings, be asked, and, if asked, shall not be required to answer, any question relating to his past which cannot be answered without acknowledging or referring to a spent conviction or spent convictions or any circumstances ancillary thereto.

(2) Subject to the provisions of any order made under subsection (4) below, where a question seeking information with respect to a person's previous convictions, offences, conduct or circumstances is put to him or to any other person otherwise than in proceedings before a judicial authority –

(a) the question shall be treated as not relating to spent convictions or to any circumstances ancillary to spent convictions, and the answer thereto may be framed accordingly; and

(b) the person questioned shall not be subjected to any liability or otherwise prejudiced in law by reason of any failure to acknowledge or disclose a spent conviction or any circumstances ancillary to a spent conviction in his answer to the question.

(3) Subject to the provisions of any order made under subsection (4) below, –

(a) any obligation imposed on any person by any rule of law or by the provisions of any agreement or arrangement to disclose any matters to any other person shall not extend to requiring him to disclose a spent conviction or any circumstances ancillary to a spent conviction (whether the conviction is his own or another's); and

(b) a conviction which has become spent or any circumstances ancillary thereto, or any failure to disclose a spent conviction or any such circumstances, shall not be a proper ground for dismissing or excluding a person from any office, profession, occupation or employment, or for prejudicing him in any way in any occupation or employment.

(4) The Secretary of State may by order –

(a) make such provisions as seems to him appropriate for excluding or modifying the application of either or both of paragraphs (a) and (b) of subsection (2) above in relation to questions put in such circumstances as may be specified in the order;

(b) provide for such exceptions from the provisions of subsection (3) above as seem to him appropriate, in such cases or classes of case, and in relation to convictions of such a description, as may be specified in the order.

(5) For the purposes of this section and section 7 below any of the following are circumstances ancillary to a conviction, that is to say –

(a) the offence or offences which were the subject of that conviction;

(b) the conduct constituting that offence or those offences; and

(c) any process or proceedings preliminary to that conviction, any sentence imposed in respect of that conviction, any proceedings (whether by way of appeal or otherwise) for reviewing that conviction or any such sentence, and anything done in pursuance of or undergone in compliance with any such sentence.

(6) For the purpose of this section and section 7 below "proceedings before a judicial authority " includes, in addition to proceedings before any of the ordinary courts of law, proceedings before any tribunal, body or person having power –

(a) by virtue of any enactment, law, custom or practice;

(b) under the rules governing any association, institution, profession, occupation or employment; or

(c) under any provision of an agreement providing for arbitration with respect to questions arising thereunder;

to determine any question affecting the rights, privileges, obligations or liabilities of any person, or to receive evidence affecting the determination of any such question.

[**Commentary**]

Rehabilitated person; spent conviction: see s 1.
Conviction: partially defined in s 1(4).
Proceedings before a judicial authority: see subs (6).

5. Rehabilitation periods for particular sentences

(As amended by the Criminal Justice Act 1982, s 77, Sch 14, s 78, Sch 16; the Criminal Justice (Scotland) Act 1980, s 83(2), Sch 7; the Armed Forces Act 1976, s 22(5), Sch 9; the Armed Forces Act 1981, s 28(1), Sch 4; the Mental Health (Amendment) Act 1982, s 65(1), Sch 3.)

(1) The sentences excluded from rehabilitation under this Act are –

(a) a sentence of imprisonment for life;

(b) a sentence of imprisonment, youth custody or corrective training for a term exceeding thirty months;

(c) a sentence of preventive detention;

(d) a sentence of detention during Her Majesty's pleasure or for life, or under section 205(2) or (3) of the Criminal Procedure (Scotland) Act 1975, or for a term exceeding thirty months, passed under section 53 of the Children and Young Persons Act 1933 (young offenders convicted of grave crimes) or under section 206 of the said Act of 1975 (detention of children convicted on indictment) or a corresponding court-martial punishment; and

(e) a sentence of custody for life

and any other sentence is a sentence subject to rehabilitation under this Act.

(1A) In subsection (1)(d) above "corresponding court-martial punishment" means a punishment awarded under section 71A(3) or (4) of the Army Act 1955, section 71A(3) or (4) of the Air Force Act 1955 or section 43A(3) or (4) of the Naval Discipline Act 1957.

(2) For the purposes of this Act –

(a) the rehabilitation period applicable to a sentence specified in the first column of Table A below is the period specified in the second column of that Table in relation to that sentence, or, where the sentence was imposed on a person who was under seventeen years of age at the date of his conviction, half that period; and

(b) the rehabilitation period applicable to a sentence specified in the first column of Table B below is the period specified in the second column of that Table in relation to that sentence;

reckoned in either case from the date of the conviction in respect of which the sentence was imposed.

TABLE A

Rehabilitation periods subject to reduction by half for persons under 17

Sentence	Rehabilitation period
A sentence of imprisonment or youth custody or corrective training for a term exceeding six months but not exceeding thirty months.	Ten years.
A sentence of cashiering, discharge with ignominy or dismissal with disgrace from Her Majesty's service.	Ten years.
A sentence of imprisonment or youth custody for a term not exceeding six months.	Seven years.
A sentence of dismissal from Her Majesty's service.	Seven years.
Any sentence of detention in respect of a conviction in service disciplinary proceedings	Five years.
A fine or any other sentence subject to rehabilitation under this Act, not being a sentence to which Table B below or any of subsections (3) or (8) below applies.	Five years.

TABLE B

Rehabilitation periods for certain sentences confined to young offenders

Sentence	Rehabilitation period
A sentence of Borstal training.	Seven years.
A custodial order under Schedule 5A to the Army Act 1955 or the Air Force Act 1955, or under Schedule 4A to the Naval Discipline Act 1957, where the maximum period of detention specified in the order is more than six months.	Seven years.
A custodial order under section 71AA of the Army Act 1955 or the Air Force Act 1955, or under section 43AA of the Naval Discipline Act 1957, where the maximum period of detention specified in the order is more than six months	Seven years.

Sentence	Rehabilitation period
A custodial order under section 71AA of the said Acts of 1955, or section 43AA of the said Act of 1957, where the maximum period of detention specified in the order is six months or less.	Three years.
A sentence of detention for a term exceeding six months but not exceeding thirty months passed under section 53 of the said Act of 1933 or under section 206 of the Criminal Procedure (Scotland) Act 1975.	Five years.
A sentence of detention for a term not exceeding six months passed under either of those provisions.	Three years.
An order for detention in a detention centre made under section 4 of the Criminal Justice Act 1982, section 4 of the Criminal Justice Act 1961	Three years.
A custodial order under any of the Schedules to the said Acts of 1955 and 1957 mentioned above, where the maximum period of detention specified in the order is six months or less.	Three years.
A custodial order under section 71AA of the said Acts of 1955, or section 43AA of the said Act of 1957, where the maximum period of detention specified in the order is six months or less.	Three years.

(3) The rehabilitation period applicable –

(a) to an order discharging a person absolutely for an offence; and

(b) to the discharge by a children's hearing under section 43(2) of the Social Work (Scotland) Act 1968 of the referral of a child's case;

shall be six months from the date of conviction.

(4) Where in respect of a conviction a person was conditionally discharged, bound over to keep the peace or be of good behaviour, or placed on probation, the rehabilitation period applicable to the sentence shall be one year from the date of conviction or a period beginning with that date and ending when the order for conditional discharge or probation order or (as the case may be) the recognisance or bond of caution to keep the peace or be of good behaviour ceases or ceased to have effect, whichever is the longer.

(5) Where in respect of a conviction any of the following sentences was imposed, that is to say –

(a) an order under section 57 of the Children and Young Persons Act 1933 or section 61 of the Children and Young Persons (Scotland) Act 1937 committing the person convicted to the care of a fit person;

(b) a supervision order under any provision of either of those Acts or of the Children and Young Persons Act 1963;

(c) an order under section 413 of the Criminal Procedure (Scotland) Act 1975 committing a child for the purpose of his undergoing residential training;

(d) an approved school order under section 61 of the said Act of 1937;

(e) a care order or a supervision order under any provision of the Children and Young Persons Act 1969; or

(f) a supervision requirement under any provision of the Social Work (Scotland) Act 1968;

(g) a community supervision order under Schedule 5A to the Army Act 1955 or the Air Force Act 1955, or under Schedule 4A to the Naval Discipline Act 1957; or

(h) a reception order under any on those Schedules,

the rehabilitation period applicable to the sentence shall be one year from the date of conviction or a period beginning with that date and ending when the order or requirement ceases or ceased to have effect, whichever is the longer.

(6) Where in respect of a conviction any of the following orders was made, that is to say –

(a) an order under section 54 of the said Act of 1933 committing the person convicted to custody in a remand home;

(b) an approved school order under section 57 of the said Act of 1933; or

(c) an attendance centre order under section 19 of the Criminal Justice Act 1948;

the rehabilitation period applicable to the sentence shall be a period beginning with the date of conviction and ending one year after the date on which the order ceases or ceased to have effect.

(7) Where in respect of a conviction a hospital order under Part III of the Mental Health Act 1983 or under Part VI of the Mental Health (Scotland) Act 1984 (with or without a restriction order) was made, the rehabilitation period applicable to the sentence shall be the period of five years from the date of conviction or a period beginning with that date and ending two years after the date on which the hospital order ceases or ceased to have effect, whichever is the longer.

(8) Where in respect of a conviction a hospital order under Part III of the Mental Health Act 1983 or under Part VI of the Mental Health (Scotland) Act 1984 (with or without a restriction order) was made imposing on the person convicted any disqualification, disability, prohibition or other penalty, the rehabilitation period applicable to the sentence shall be a period beginning with the date of conviction and ending on the date on which the disqualification, disability, prohibition or penalty (as the case may be) ceases or ceased to have effect.

(9) For the purposes of this section –

(a) "sentence of imprisonment" includes a sentence of detention under section 207 or 415 of the Criminal Procedure (Scotland) Act 1975 and a sentence of penal servitude, and "term of imprisonment" shall be construed accordingly;

(b) consecutive terms of imprisonment or of detention under section 53 of the said Act of 1933 or section 206 of the said Act of 1975, and terms which are wholly or partly concurrent (being terms of imprisonment or detention imposed in respect of offences of which a person was convicted in the same proceedings) shall be treated as a single term;

(c) no account shall be taken of any subsequent variation, made by a court in dealing with a person in respect of a suspended sentence of imprisonment, of the term originally imposed; and

(d) a sentence imposed by a court outside Great Britain shall be treated as a sentence of that one of the descriptions mentioned in this section which most nearly corresponds to the sentence imposed.

(10) References in this section to the period during which a probation order, or a care order or supervision order under the Children and Young Persons Act 1969, or a supervision requirement under the Social Work (Scotland) Act 1968, is or was in force include references to any period during which any order or requirement to which this subsection applies, being an order or requirement made or imposed directly or indirectly in substitution for the first-mentioned order or requirement, is or was in force.

This subsection applies –

(a) to any such order or requirement as is mentioned above in this subsection;

(b) to any order having effect under section 25(2) of the said Act of 1969 as if it were a training school order in Northern Ireland; and

(c) to any supervision order made under section 72(2) of the said Act of 1968 and having effect as a supervision order under the Children and Young Persons Act (Northern Ireland) 1950.

(10A) The reference in subsection (5) above to the period during which a reception order has effect includes a reference to any subsequent period during which by virtue of the order having been made the Social Work (Scotland) Act 1968 or the Children and Young Persons Act (Northern Ireland) 1968 has effect in relation to the person in respect of whom the order was made and subsection (10) above shall accordingly have effect in relation to any such subsequent period.

(11) The Secretary of State may by order –

(a) substitute different periods or terms for any of the periods or terms mentioned in subsections (1) to (8) above; and

(b) substitute a different age for the age mentioned in subsection (2)(a) above.

[**Commentary**]

Seventeen years of age: a person attains a given age at the commencement of the relevant anniversary of his birth: Family Law Reform Act 1969, s 9.

Sentence of imprisonment: see subs (9)(a).

Subsection (11): no orders have been made under this subsection.

6. The rehabilitation period applicable to a conviction

(As amended by the Criminal Law Act 1977, s 65(4), Sch 12; the Magistrates' Courts Act 1980, s 154, Sch7.)

(1) Where only one sentence is imposed in respect of a conviction (not being a sentence excluded from rehabilitation under this Act) the rehabilitation period applicable to the conviction is, subject to the following provisions of this section, the period applicable to the sentence in accordance with section 5 above.

(2) Where more than once sentence is imposed in respect of a conviction (whether or not in the same proceedings) and none of the sentences imposed is excluded from rehabilitation under this Act, then, subject to the following provisions of this section, if the periods applicable to those sentences in accordance with section 5 above differ, the rehabilitation period applicable to the conviction shall be the longer or the longest (as the case may be) of those periods.

(3) Without prejudice to subsection (2) above, where in respect of a conviction a person was conditionally discharged or placed on probation and after the end of the rehabilitation period applicable to the conviction in accordance with subsection (1) or (2) above he is dealt with, in consequence of a breach of conditional discharge or

probation, for the offence for which the order for conditional discharge or probation order was made, then, if the rehabilitation period applicable to the conviction in accordance with subsection (2) above (taking into account any sentence imposed when he is so dealt with) ends later than the rehabilitation period previously applicable to the conviction, he shall be treated for the purposes of this Act as not having become a rehabilitated person in respect of that conviction, and the conviction shall for those purposes be treated as not having become spent, in relation to any period falling before the end of the new rehabilitation period.

(4) Subject to subsection (5) below, where during the rehabilitation period applicable to a conviction –

(a) the person convicted is convicted of a further offence; and

(b) no sentence excluded from rehabilitation under this Act is imposed on him in respect of the later conviction;

if the rehabilitation period applicable in accordance with this section to either of the convictions would end earlier than the period so applicable in relation to the other, the rehabilitation period which would (apart from this subsection) end the earlier shall be extended so as to end at the same time as the other rehabilitation period.

(5) Where the rehabilitation period applicable to a conviction is the rehabilitation period in accordance with section 5(8) above to an order imposing on a person any disqualification, disability, prohibition or other penalty, the rehabilitation period applicable to another conviction shall not by virtue by subsection (4) above be extended by reference to that period; but if any other sentence is imposed in respect of the first-mentioned conviction for which a rehabilitation period is prescribed by any other provision of section 5 above, the rehabilitation period applicable to another conviction shall, where appropriate be extended under subsection (4) above by reference to the rehabilitation period applicable in accordance with that section to that sentence or, where more than one such

sentence is imposed, by reference to the longer or longest of the periods so applicable to those sentences, as if the period in question were the rehabilitation period applicable to the first-mentioned conviction.

(6) Subject to subsection (7) below, for the purposes of subsection (4)(a) above there shall be disregarded–

(a) any conviction in England and Wales of a summary offence or of a scheduled offence (within the meaning of section 22 of the Magistrates' Courts Act 1980, tried summarily in pursuance of subsection (2) of that section (summary trial where value involved is small);

(b) any conviction in Scotland of an offence which is not excluded from the jurisdiction of inferior courts of summary jurisdiction by virtue of section 4 of the Summary Jurisdiction (Scotland) Act 1954 (certain crimes not to be tried in inferior courts of summary jurisdiction); and

(c) any conviction by or before a court outside Great Britain of an offence in respect of conduct which, if it had taken place in any part of Great Britain, would not have constituted an offence under the law in force in that part of Great Britain.

(7) Notwithstanding subsection (6) above, a conviction in service disciplinary proceedings shall not be disregarded for the purposes of subsection (4)(a) above.

[**Commentary**]

Sentence: partially defined in s 1(3).
Conviction: partially defined in s 1(4).
A sentence excluded from rehabilitation: see s 5(1).
Rehabilitation period: see s 5.

7. Limitations on rehabilitation under this Act, etc

(As amended by the Banking Act 1979, s 43(4).)

(1) Nothing in section 4(1) above shall affect –

(a) any right of Her Majesty, by virtue of Her Royal

prerogative or otherwise, to grant a free pardon, to quash any conviction or sentence, or to commute any sentence;

(b) the enforcement by any process or proceedings of any fine or other sum adjudged to be paid by or imposed on a spent conviction;

(c) the issue of any process for the purpose of proceedings in respect of any breach of a condition or requirement applicable to a sentence imposed in respect of a spent conviction; or

(d) the operation of any enactment by virtue of which, in consequence of any conviction, a person is subject, otherwise than by way of sentence, to any disqualification, disability, prohibition or other penalty the period of which extends beyond the rehabilitation period applicable in accordance with section 6 above to the conviction.

(2) Nothing in section 4(1) above shall affect the determination of any issue, or prevent the admission or requirement of any evidence, relating to a person's previous convictions or to circumstances ancillary thereto –

(a) in any criminal proceedings before a court in Great Britain (including any appeal or reference in a criminal matter);

(b) in any service disciplinary proceedings or in any proceedings on appeal from any service disciplinary proceedings;

(c) in any proceedings relating to adoption or to the guardianship, wardship, marriage, custody, care or control of, or access to, any minor, or to the provision by any person of accommodation, care or schooling for minors;

(d) in any care proceedings under section 1 of the Children and Young Persons Act 1969 or on appeal from any such proceedings, or in any proceedings relating to the variation or discharge of a care order or supervision order under that Act;

(e) in any proceedings before a children's hearing under the Social Work (Scotland) Act 1968 or on appeal from any such hearing; or

(f) in any proceedings in which he is a party or a witness, provided that, on the occasion when the issue or the admission or requirement of the evidence falls to be determined, he consents to the determination of the issue or, as the case may be, the admission or requirement of the evidence notwithstanding the provisions of section 4(1); or

(g) in any proceedings arising out of any such decision of the Bank of England as is referred to in section 11(1) of the Banking Act 1979, including proceedings on appeal to any court.

In the application of this subsection to Scotland, "minor" means a child under the age of eighteen, including a pupil child.

(3) If at any stage in any proceedings before a judicial authority in Great Britain (not being proceedings to which, by virtue of any of paragraphs (a) to (e) of subsection (2) above or of any order for the time being in force under subsection (4) below, section 4(1) above has no application, or proceedings to which section 8 below applies) the authority is satisfied, in the light of any considerations which appear to it to be relevant (including any evidence which has been or may thereafter be put before it), that justice cannot be done in the case except by admitting or requiring evidence relating to a person's spent convictions or to circumstances ancillary thereto, that authority may admit or, as the case may be, require the evidence in question notwithstanding the provisions of subsection (1) of section 4 above, and may determine any issue to which the evidence relates in disregard, so far as necessary, of those provisions.

(4) The Secretary of State may by order exclude the application of section 4(1) above in relation to any proceedings specified in the order (other than proceedings to which section 8 below applies) to such extent and for such purposes as may be so specified.

(5) No order made by a court with respect to any person otherwise than on a conviction shall be included in any list or statement of that person's previous convictions given or made to any court which is considering how to deal with him in respect of any offence.

[**Commentary**]

Sentence: partially defined in s 1(3).
Circumstances ancillary thereto: defined in s 4(5).
Minor: a person under eighteen years of age: Family Law Reform Act 1969, s 1(1).
Proceedings before a judicial authority: partially defined in s 4(6).

8. Defamation actions

(1) This section applies to any action for libel or slander begun after the commencement of this Act by a rehabilitated person and founded upon the publication of any matter imputing that the plaintiff has committed or been charged with or prosecuted for or convicted of or sentenced for an offence which was the subject of a spent conviction.

(2) Nothing in section 4(1) above shall affect an action to which this section applies where the publication complained of took place before the conviction in question became spent, and the following provisions of this section shall not apply in any such case.

(3) Subject to subsections (5) and (6) below, nothing in section 4(1) above shall prevent the defendant in an action to which this section applies from relying on any defence of justification or fair comment or of absolute or qualified privilege which is available to him, or restrict the matters he may establish in support of any such defence.

(4) Without prejudice to the generality of subsection (3) above, where in any such action malice is alleged against a defendant who is relying on a defence of qualified privilege, nothing in section 4(1) above shall restrict the matters he may establish in rebuttal of the allegation.

(5) A defendant in any such action shall not by virtue of

subsection (3) above be entitled to rely upon the defence of justification if the publication is proved to have been made with malice.

(6) Subject to subsection (7) below a defendant in any such action shall not, by virtue of subsection (3) above, be entitled to rely on any matter or adduce or require any evidence for the purpose of establishing (whether under section 3 of the Law of Libel Amendment Act 1888 or otherwise) the defence that the matter published constituted a fair and accurate report of judicial proceedings if it is proved that the publication contained a reference to evidence which was ruled to be inadmissible in the proceedings by virtue of section 4(1) above.

(7) Subsection (3) above shall apply without the qualifications imposed by subsection (6) above in relation to –

(a) any report of judicial proceedings contained in any bona fide series of law reports which does not form part of any other publication and consists solely of reports of proceedings in courts of law; and

(b) any report or account of judicial proceedings published for bona fide educational, scientific or professional purposes, or given in the course of any lecture, class or discussion given or held for any of those purposes.

(8) In the application of this section to Scotland –

(a) for the reference in subsection (1) to libel and slander there shall be substituted a reference to defamation;

(b) for references to the plaintiff and the defendant there shall be substituted respectively references to the pursuer and the defender; and

(c) for references to the defence of justification there shall be substituted references to the defence of veritas.

[**Commentary**]

Commencement of this Act: 1 July 1975.
Convicted; sentenced: partially defined in s 1(4), (3).
Rehabilitated person: see s 5.

9. Unauthorized disclosure of spent convictions
(As amended by the Criminal Justice Act 1982, ss 38, 46.)

(1) In this section –

"official record" means a record kept for the purposes of its functions by any court, police force, Government department, local or other public authority in Great Britain, or a record kept, in Great Britain or elsewhere, for the purposes of any of Her Majesty's forces, being in either case a record containing information about persons convicted of offences; and

"specified information" means information imputing that a named or otherwise identifiable rehabilitated living person has committed or been charged with or prosecuted for or convicted of or sentenced for any offence which is the subject of a spent conviction.

(2) Subject to the provisions of any order made under subsection (5) below, any person who, in the course of his official duties, has or at any time has had custody of or access to any official record or the information contained therein, shall be guilty of an offence if, knowing or having reasonable cause to suspect that any specified information he has obtained in the course of those duties is specified information, he discloses it, otherwise than in the course of those duties, to another person.

(3) In any proceedings for an offence under subsection (2) above it shall be a defence for the defendant (or, in Scotland, the accused person) to show that the disclosure was made –

(a) to the rehabilitated person or to another person at the express request of the rehabilitated person; or

(b) to a person whom he reasonably believed to be the rehabilitated person or to another person at the express request of a person whom he reasonably believed to be the rehabilitated person.

(4) Any person who obtains any specified information

from any official record by means of any fraud, dishonesty or bribe shall be guilty of an offence.

(5) The Secretary of State may by order make such provision as appears to him to be appropriate for excepting the disclosure of specified information derived from an official record from the provisions of subsection (2) above in such cases or classes of case as may be specified in the order.

(6) Any person guilty of an offence under subsection (2) above shall be liable on summary conviction to a fine not exceeding level 4 on the standard scale.

(7) Any person guilty of an offence under subsection (4) above shall be liable on summary conviction to a fine not exceeding level 5 on the standard scale or to imprisonment for a term not exceeding six months, or to both.

(8) Proceedings for an offence under subsection (2) above shall not, in England and Wales, be instituted except by or on behalf of the Director of Public Prosecutions.

[**Commentary**]

Convicted: see s 1(4).
Sentenced: partially defined in s 1(3).
The standard scale: defined in the Criminal Justice Act 1982, ss 37(3), 75 as the standard scale set out in s 37(2) of that Act, as amended by Order.

10. Orders

(1) Any power of the Secretary of State to make an order under any provision of this Act shall be exercisable by statutory instrument, and an order made under any provision of this Act except section 11 below may be varied or revoked by a subsequent order made under that provision.

(2) No order shall be made by the Secretary of State under any provision of this Act other than section 11 below unless a draft of it has been laid before, and approved by resolution of, each House of Parliament.

11. Citation, commencement and extent

(1) This Act may be cited as the Rehabilitation of Offenders Act 1974.

(2) This Act shall come into force on 1st July 1975 or such earlier day as the Secretary of State may by order appoint.

(3) This Act shall not apply to Northern Ireland.

Appendix 2

The Rehabilitation of Offenders Act 1974 (Exceptions) Order 1975
(SI 1975 No. 1023)

(As amended by SI 1986 Nos 1249 and 2268.)

1. This Order may be cited as the Rehabilitation of Offenders Act 1974 (Exceptions) Order 1975 and shall come into operation on 1st July 1975.

2.–(1) In this Order, except where the context otherwise requires –

"the Act" means the Rehabilitation of Offenders Act 1974;

"the Building Societies Commission" means the Building Societies Commission established by section 1 of the Building Societies Act 1986;

"relevant offence" means

(a) an offence involving fraud or other dishonesty; or

(b) an offence under legislation (whether or not of the United Kingdom) relating to building societies, companies (including insider dealing), industrial and provident societies, credit unions, friendly societies, insurance, banking or other financial services, insolvency, consumer credit or consumer protection;

the expressions "authorisation", "building society" and "officer" have the meanings respectively given to them by section 119(1) of the Building Societies Act 1986.

(2) Where, by virtue of this Order, the operation of any of the provisions of the Act is excluded in relation to spent convictions the exclusion shall be taken to extend to spent convictions for offences of every description unless the said

provisions are excluded only in relation to spent convictions for relevant offences.

(3) Part IV of Schedule 1 to this Order shall have effect for the interpretation of expressions used in that Schedule.

(4) In this Order a reference to any enactment shall be construed as a reference to that enactment as amended, extended or applied by or under any other enactment.

(5) The Interpretation Act 1889 shall apply to the interpretation of this Order as it applies to the interpretation of an Act of Parliament.

3. None of the provisions of section 4(2) of the Act shall apply in relation to –

(a) any question asked by or on behalf of any person, in the course of the duties of his office or employment, in order to assess the suitability –

(i) of the person to whom the question relates for admission to any of the professions specified in Part I of Schedule 1 to this Order; or

(ii) of the person to whom the question relates for any office or employment specified in Part II of the said Schedule 1; or

(iii) of the person to whom the question relates or of any other person to pursue any occupation specified in Part III of the said Schedule 1 or to pursue it subject to a particular condition or restriction; or

(iv) of the person to whom the question relates or of any other person to hold a licence, certificate or permit of a kind specified in Schedule 2 to this Order or to hold it subject to a particular condition or restriction,

where the person questioned is informed at the time the question is asked that, by virtue of this Order, spent convictions are to be disclosed;

(aa) any question asked by or on behalf of any person, in the course of the duties of his office or employment, in order to assess the suitability of another person for any office or employment specified in paragraph 14 of Part II of the said Schedule 1 or the suitability of another person to be concerned, otherwise than in the course of the duties of his office or employment, with such provision as is mentioned in that paragraph, if –

(i) the question relates to that other person and the said provision would normally enable that other person to have access to the persons referred to in that paragraph; or

(ii) the question relates to a person who lives in the same household as that other person and the said provision would normally take place in that household,

where the person questioned is informed at the time the question is asked that, by virtue of this Order, spent convictions are to be disclosed;

(ab) any question relating to a relevant offence which is put by or on behalf of the Building Societies Commission or a building society in order to assess the suitability of the person to whom the question relates to be a director or other officer of a building society, whether or not that individual is the person questioned and where the person questioned is informed at the time the question is asked that, by virtue of this Order, spent convictions for any relevant offence are to be disclosed;

(b) any office, employment or occupation specified in Part II or his duties as a person employed in the service of the Crown, the United Kingdom Atomic Energy Authority, the Civil Aviation Authority or the Post Office Corporation, in order to assess, for the purpose of safeguarding national security, the suitability of the person to whom the question relates or of any other person for any office or employment where the person questioned is informed at the time the question is asked that, by virtue of this Order, spent convictions are to be disclosed for the purpose of safeguarding national security.

4. Paragraph (b) of section 4(3) of the Act shall not apply in relation to –

(a) the dismissal or exclusion of any person from any profession specified in Part I of Schedule 1 to this Order;

(b) any office, employment or occupation specified in Part II or Part III of the said Schedule 1;

(c) any action taken for the purpose of safeguarding national security.

(d) any of the following, that is to say –

(i) the refusal by the Building Societies Commission to grant authorisation;

(ii) the revocation by the said Commission of a building society's authorisation;

(iii) the imposition by the said Commission of conditions on its authorisation;

(iv) the dismissal or exclusion by a building society of a person from a position as an officer in a building society,

by reason, or partly by reason, of a spent conviction of an individual for a relevant offence, or of any circumstances ancillary to such a conviction or of a failure (whether or not by that individual) to disclose such a conviction or any such circumstances.

5.–(1) Section 4(1) of the Act shall not

(a) apply in relation to any proceedings specified in Schedule 3 to this Order;

(b) apply in relation to any proceedings specified in paragraph (2) below to the extent that there falls to be determined therein any issue relating to a person's spent conviction for any relevant offence or to circumstances ancillary thereto:

(c) prevent, in any proceedings specified in paragraph (2) below, the admission or requirement of any evidence relating to a person's spent conviction for any relevant offence or to circumstances ancillary thereto.

(2) The proceedings referred to in paragraph (1) above are –

(a) any proceedings before the Building Societies Commission –

(i) on an application for authorisation;

(ii) for the revocation of authorisation, or

(iii) for the imposition of conditions on authorisations, as to the conditions imposed or as to their revocation; and

(b) any proceedings by way of appeal against, or review of, any decision taken by the said Commission following any proceedings falling within sub-paragraph (a) above.

Roy Jenkins,
One of Her Majesty's Principal
Secretaries of State
Home Office,
Whitehall.

SCHEDULE 1

(Articles 2(3), 3 and 4)
Excepted Professions, Offices, Employments and Occupations

Part 1

Professions

1. Medical practitioner.
2. Barrister (in England and Wales), advocate (in Scotland), solicitor.
3. Chartered accountant, certified accountant.
4. Dentist, dental hygenist, dental auxiliary.
5. Veterinary surgeon.
6. Nurse, midwife.
7. Ophthalmic optician, dispensing optician.
8. Pharmaceutical chemist.
9. Registered teacher (in Scotland).
10. Any profession to which the Professions Supplementary to Medicine Act 1960 applies and which is undertaken following registration under that Act.

Part II

Offices and employments

1. Judicial appointments.
2. The Director of Public Prosecutions and any employment in his office.
3. Procurators Fiscal and District Court Prosecutors, and any employment in the office of a Procurator Fiscal or District Court Prosecutor or in the Crown Office.
4. Justices' clerks and their assistants.
5. Clerks (including depute and assistant clerks) and officers of the High Court of Justiciary, the Court of Session and the district court, sheriff clerks (including sheriff clerks depute) and their clerks and assistants.
6. Constables, persons appointed as police cadets to undergo training with a view to becoming constables and persons employed for the purposes of, or to assist the constables of, a police force established under any enactment; naval, military and air force police.
7. Any employment which is concerned with the administration of, or is otherwise normally carried out wholly or partly within the precincts of, a prison, remand centre, detention centre, Borstal institution or young offenders institution, and members of boards of visitors appointed under section 6 of the Prison Act 1952 or of visiting committees appointed under section 7 of the Prisons (Scotland) Act 1952.
8. Traffic wardens appointed under section 81 of the Road Traffic Regulation Act 1967 or section 9 of the Police (Scotland) Act 1967.
9. Probation officers appointed under Schedule 3 to the Powers of Criminal Courts Act 1973.

....

12. Any employment by a local authority in connection with the provisions of social services or by any other body in connection with the provision by it of similar services, being employment which is of such a kind as

to enable the holder to have access to any of the following classes of person in the course of his normal duties, namely –

(a) persons over the age of 65;

(b) persons suffering from serious illness or mental disorder of any description;

(c) persons addicted to alcohol or drugs;

(d) persons who are blind, deaf or dumb;

(e) other persons who are substantially and permanently handicapped by illness, injury or congenital deformity.

13. Any employment which is concerned with the provision of health services and which is of such a kind as to enable the holder to have access to persons in receipt of such services in the course of his normal duties.

14. Any office or employment concerned with the provision to persons aged under 18 of accommodation, care, leisure and recreational facilities, schooling, social services, supervision or training, being an office or employment of such a kind as to enable the holder to have access in the course of his normal duties to such persons, and any other office or employment the normal duties of which are carried out wholly or partly on the premises where such provision takes place.

Part III

Regulated occupations

1. Firearms dealer.

2. Any occupation in respect of which an application to the Gaming Board for Great Britain for a licence, certificate or registration is required by or under any enactment.

3. Director, controller or manager of an insurance company –

(a) in respect of which the Secretary of State's

authorisation is required under section 3(1)(b) of the Insurance Companies Act 1974 for it to carry on insurance business; or

(b) to which Part II of that Act applies.

....

6. Any occupation which is concerned with –

(a) the management of a place in respect of which the approval of the Secretary of State is required by section 1 of the Abortion Act 1967; or

(b) in England and Wales, carrying on a nursing home in respect of which registration is required by section 187 of the Public Health Act 1936 or section 14 of the Mental Health Act 1959; or

(c) in Scotland, carrying on a nursing home in respect of which registration is required under section 1 of the Nursing Homes Registration (Scotland) Act 1938 or a private hospital in respect of which registration is required under section 15 of the Mental Health (Scotland) Act 1960.

7. Any occupation which is concerned with carrying on an establishment in respect of which registration is required by section 37 of the National Assistance Act 1948 or section 61 of the Social Work (Scotland) Act 1968.

8. Any occupation in respect of which the holder, as occupier of premises on which explosives are kept, is required by an Order in Council made under section 43 of the Explosives Act 1875 to obtain from the police or a court of summary jurisdiction a certificate as to his fitness to keep the explosives.

Part IV

Interpretation

In this schedule –

"certified accountant" means a member of the Association of Certified Accountants;

"chartered accountant" means a member of the Institute of Chartered Accountants in England and Wales or of the

Institute of Chartered Accountants of Scotland.

"firearms dealer" has the meaning assigned to that expression by section 57(4) of the Firearms Act 1968.

"further education" has the meaning assigned to that expression by section 41 of the Education Act 1944 or, in Scotland, section 4 of the Education (Scotland) Act 1962.

"health services" means services provided under the National Health Service Acts 1946 to 1973 or the National Health Service (Scotland) Acts 1947 to 1973 and similar services provided otherwise than under the National Health Service;

"insurance company" has the meaning assigned to that expression by section 85 of the Insurance Companies Act 1974 and, in relation to an insurance company "director" shall be construed in accordance with that section and "controller" and "manager" shall be construed in accordance with section 7 of that Act;

"judicial appointment" means an appointment to any office by virtue of which the holder has power (whether alone or with others) under any enactment or rule of law to determine any question affecting the rights, privileges, obligations or liabilities of any person;

"proprietor" and "independent school" have the meanings assigned to those expressions by section 114(1) of the Education Act 1944 or, in Scotland, section 145 of the Education (Scotland) Act 1962;

"registered teacher" means a teacher registered under the Teaching Council (Scotland) Act 1965 and includes a provisionally registered teacher;

"school" has the meaning assigned to that expression by section 114(1) of the Education Act 1944 or, in Scotland, section 145 of the Education (Scotland) Act 1962;

"social services", in relation to a local authority, means –

(a) in England and Wales, services provided by the authority in discharging its social services functions within the meaning of the Local Authority Social Services Act 1970;

(b) in Scotland, services provided by the authority in

discharging functions referred to in section 2(2) of the Social Work (Scotland) Act 1968;

"teacher" includes a warden of a community centre, leader of a youth club or similar institution, youth worker and, in Scotland, youth and community worker.

(Article 3)

SCHEDULE 2

Excepted Licences, Certificates and Permits

1. Firearm certificates and shot gun certificates issued under the Firearms Act 1968, and permits issued under section 7(1), 9(2) or 13(1)(c) of that Act.

2. Licences issued under section 25 of the Children and Young Persons Act 1933 (which relates to persons under the age of 18 going abroad for the purpose of performing or being exhibited for profit).

3. Certificates issued by the police or a court of summary jurisdiction under any Order in Council made under section 43 of the Explosives Act 1875 as to the fitness of a person to keep explosives for private use.

(Article 5)

SCHEDULE 3

Excepted Proceedings

1. Proceedings in respect of a person's admission to, or disciplinary proceedings against a member of, any profession specified in Part I of Schedule 1 to this Order.

2. Proceedings before the Court of Appeal or the High Court in the exercise of their disciplinary jurisdiction in respect of solicitors.

3. Disciplinary proceedings against a constable.

4. Proceedings before the Gaming Board for Great Britain.

5. Proceedings under the Mental Health Act 1959 before any Mental Health Review Tribunal, or under the Mental Health (Scotland) Act 1960 before the Sheriff or the Mental Welfare Commission for Scotland.

6. Proceedings under the Firearms Act 1968 in respect of –

(a) the registration of a person as a firearms dealer, the removal of a person's name from a register of firearms dealers or the imposition, variation or revocation of conditions of any such registration; or

(b) the grant, renewal, variation or revocation of a firearm certificate; or

(c) the grant, renewal or revocation of a shot gun certificate; or

(d) the grant of a permit under section 7(1), 9(2) or 13(1)(c) of that Act.

7. Proceedings in respect of the grant, renewal or variation of a licence under section 25 of the Children and Young Persons Act 1933 (which relates to persons under the age of 18 going abroad for the purpose of performing or being exhibited for profit).

8. Proceedings –

(a) in respect of an application under section 3(1)(b) of the Insurance Companies Act 1974 for the Secretary of State's authorisation to carry on insurance business; or

(b) in respect of a notice under section 38 or 39 of that Act (which relate to notification of the proposed exercise of certain powers conferred by the Act on the Secretary of State) or

(c) under section 52 or 53 of that Act (which relate to the Secretary of State's approval of appointments in insurance companies).

9. Proceedings in respect of a determination by the Secretary of State as to the suitability of a person –

(a) for employment as a teacher in a school or establishment for further education (within the meaning of paragraph 10 of Part II of Schedule 1 to this Order), or in determining the extent to which a person may be employed as such a teacher; or

(b) to be the proprietor of an independent school

(within the meaning of paragraph 11 of the said Part II), (including proceedings before an independent Schools Tribunal in respect of the above matters under section 72 of the Education Act 1944 or section 113 of the Education (Scotland) Act 1963).

11. Proceedings in respect of an application for, or cancellation of, –

(a) the Secretary of State's approval of a place under section 1 of the Abortion Act 1967; or

(b) in England and Wales, registration in respect of a nursing home under section 187 or the Public Health Act 1936 or section 14 of the Mental Health Act 1959; or

(c) in Scotland, registration in respect of a nursing home under section 1 of the Nursing Homes Registration (Scotland) Act 1938 or of a private hospital under section 15 of the Mental Health (Scotland) Act 1960.

12. Proceedings in respect of an application for, or cancellation of, registration under section 37 of the National Assistance Act 1948 or section 61 of the Social Work (Scotland) Act 1968 in respect of any such establishment as is mentioned in those sections.

13. Proceedings on an application to the police or a court of summary jurisdiction for a certificate under any Order in Council made under section 43 of the Explosives Act 1875 as to the fitness of the applicant to keep explosives.

14. Proceedings by way of appeal against, or review of, any decision taken, by virtue of any of the provisions of this Order, on consideration of a spent conviction.

15. Proceedings held for the receipt of evidence affecting the determination of any question arising in any proceedings specified in this Schedule.

Appendix 3

Financial Services Act 1986, s 189

Restriction of Rehabilitation of Offenders Act 1974

189.—(1) The Rehabilitation of Offenders Act 1974 shall have effect subject to the provisions of this section in cases where the spent conviction is for —

(a) an offence involving fraud or other dishonesty; or

(b) an offence under legislation (whether or not of the United Kingdom) relating to companies (including insider dealing), building societies, industrial and provident societies, credit unions, friendly societies, insurance, banking or other financial services, insolvency, consumer credit or consumer protection.

(2) Nothing in section 4(1) (restriction on evidence as to spent convictions in proceedings) shall prevent the determination in any proceedings specified in Part I of Schedule 14 to this Act of any issue, or prevent the admission or requirement in any such proceedings of any evidence, relating to a person's previous convictions for any such offence as is mentioned in subsection (1) above or to circumstances ancillary thereto.

(3) A conviction for any such offence as is mentioned in subsection (1) above shall not be regarded as spent for the purposes of section 4(2) (questions relating to an individual's previous convictions) if —

(a) the question is put by or on behalf of a person specified in the first column of Part II of that Schedule and relates to an individual (whether or not the person questioned) specified in relation to the person putting the question in the second column of that Part; and

(b) the person questioned is informed when the question is put that by virtue of this section convictions for any such offence are to be disclosed.

(4) Section 4(3)(b) (spent conviction not to be ground for excluding person from office, occupation etc.) shall not prevent a person specified in the first column of Part III of that Schedule from taking such action as is specified in relation to that person in the second column of that Part by reason, or partly by reason, of a spent conviction for any such offence as is mentioned in subsection (1) above of an individual who is –

(a) the person in respect of whom the action is taken;

(b) as respects action within paragraph 1 or 4 of that Part, an associate of that person; or

(c) as respects action within paragraph 1 of that Part consisting of a decision to refuse or revoke an order declaring a collective investment scheme to be an authorised unit trust scheme or a recognised scheme, the operator or trustee of the scheme or an associate of his,

or of any circumstances ancillary to such a conviction or of a failure (whether or not by that individual) to disclose such a conviction or any such circumstances.

(5) Parts I, II and III of that Schedule shall have effect subject to Part IV.

(6) In this section and that Schedule "associate" means –

(a) in relation to a body corporate, a director, manager or controller;

(b) in relation to a partnership, a partner or manager;

(c) in relation to a registered friendly society, a trustee, manager or member of the committee of the society;

(d) in relation to an unincorporated association, a member of its governing body or an officer, manager or controller;

(e) in relation to an individual, a manager.

(7) This section and that Schedule shall apply to Northern Ireland with the substitution for the references to the said Act of 1974 and section 4(1), (2) and (3)(b) of that Act of references to the Rehabilitation of Offenders (Northern Ireland) Order 1978 and Article 5(1), (2) and 3(b) of that Order.

Appendix 4

The Banking Act 1987, s 95

Restriction of Rehabilitation of Offenders Act 1974

95.–(1) The Rehabilitation of Offenders Act 1974 shall have effect subject to the provisions of this section in cases where the spent conviction is for –

(a) an offence involving fraud or other dishonesty; or

(b) an offence under legislation (whether or not of the United Kingdom) relating to companies (including insider dealing), building societies, industrial and provident societies, credit unions, friendly societies, insurance, banking or other financial services, insolvency, consumer credit or consumer protection.

(2) Nothing in section 4(1) (restriction on evidence as to spent convictions in proceedings) shall prevent the determination in any proceeding arising out of any such decision of the Bank as is mentioned in section 27(1) or (3) above (including proceedings on appeal to any court) of any issue, or prevent the admission or requirement in any such proceedings of any evidence, relating to a person's previous convictions for any such offence as is mentioned in subsection (1) above or the circumstances ancillary thereto.

(3) A conviction for such an offence as is mentioned in subsection (1) above shall not be regarded as spent for the purposes of section 4(2) (questions relating to an individual's previous convictions) if –

(a) the question is put by or on behalf of the Bank and the individual is a person who is or is seeking to become a director, controller or manager of an authorised institution, a former authorised institution or an institution which has made an application for authorisation which has not been disposed of; or

(b) the question is put by or on behalf of such institution and the individual is or is seeking to become a director, controller or manager of that institution,

and the person questioned is informed that by virtue of this section convictions for any such offence are to be disclosed.

(4) Section 4(3)(b) (spent conviction not to be ground for excluding person from office, occupation etc.) shall not –

(a) prevent the Bank from refusing to grant or revoking an authorisation on the ground that an individual is not a fit and proper person to be a director, controller or manager of the institution in question or from imposing a restriction or giving a direction requiring the removal of an individual as director, controller or manager of an institution; or

(b) prevent an authorised institution, a former authorised institution or an institution which has made an application for authorisation which has not yet been disposed of from dismissing or excluding an individual from being a director, controller or manager of the institution,

by reason, or partly by reason, of a spent conviction of that individual for such an offence as is mentioned in subsection (1) above or any circumstances ancillary to such a conviction or of a failure (whether or not by that individual) to disclose such a conviction or any such circumstances.

(5) For the purposes of subsections (3) and (4) above an application by an institution is not disposed of until the decision of the Bank on the application is communicated to the institution.

(6) This section shall apply to Northern Ireland with the substitution for the references to the said Act of 1974 and section 4(1), (2) and (3)(b) of that Act of references to the Rehabilitation of Offenders (Northern Ireland) Order 1978 and Article 5(1), (2) and (3)(b) of that Order.

Appendix 5

The Rehabilitation of Offenders Act 1974: a historical note

In 1972 the report *Living it Down* was produced by a committee set up jointly by Justice, the Howard League for Penal Reform and NACRO under the distinguished chairmanship of Lord Gardiner. On the basis of figures prepared by the Home Office Research Unit it claimed that there were about a million people in England and Wales who had a criminal record but who had not been convicted again for at least ten years. A survey of 4,000 males arrested in London in 1957 suggested that nine out of ten of those who go straight for five years are still on the right side of the law after ten years, after which the chance of their being convicted again is minimal. Such people, said the report, are none the less faced with great difficulties, especially in the field of employment and insurance, and in the courts; however exemplary their lives may have been for many years, malice or chance may at any time put an end to their rehabilitation. It is in society's interests, the report argued, that, when someone has done all he can to live down his past, and enough time has passed to establish his sincerity, his record should no longer be held against him so long as he does not offend again. The committee took the view that the best way to encourage society to treat as rehabilitated those who have in fact rehabilitated themselves by their conduct is for the law itself to treat them in that way. The simplest means of achieving that end, they suggested, was to provide that, where a person has so rehabilitated himself, the courts will not with certain necessary exceptions admit any evidence to the contrary.

The controversy over the Bill

A Bill to give effect to these proposals was introduced into the Lords in 1972 by Lord Gardiner. It was lost with the dissolution. Equally unsuccessful was an identical Bill introduced in the Commons the following year by Mr Kenneth Marks. Finally, Mr Piers Dixon won the private members' ballot and it was the Bill over his name (though, as will be seen, not his text) which received the Royal Assent on 31 July 1974. According to Lord Gardiner, this Bill enjoyed or managed to achieve the approval of the Lord Chief Justice, Ministers in both Governments and all the relevant Government departments, the National Association of Probation Officers, the Confederation of British Industry, the British Insurance Association and many other organisations and Members of Parliament. The first real opposition to the measure was voiced by the president of the Justices' Clerks' Society in May of that year. After expressing sympathy with the motives of the Bill, he said of its provisions:

> Put shortly, they would make it a wrongful act punishable in damages for anyone, however well-intentioned, to speak the truth – and that can never be right; they would represent a shackle on the freedom of the press to comment on the careers of public persons – and in this view we are supported by the recent pronouncement of the Faulks Committee; and they would deny to the courts information which could be of assistance in determining the correct sentence in the event of any future prosecution, a matter with which we are professionally concerned.

This alerted the press and other interests, and criticisms of the Bill followed thick and fast from such varied sources as the chairman of the Bar Council, the director of APEX, the Society of Authors, the Institute of Journalists and the Guild of British Newspaper Editors. Editorial opinion against the Bill was expressed in such organs as the *Sunday Times*, the *U.K. Press Gazette* and the *New Law Journal.* Since many of the objections have been removed there seems little point in repeating them here, but the way in which this was achieved is worthy of record.

In the third reading of the Bill in the Commons in June 1974, Mr Ivor Stanbrook protested that the Government amendments put down in standing committee:

> were complex and amounted to a complete rewriting of the whole Bill, in that the original clauses were all deleted and fresh clauses were proposed. Those amendments were put down only 48 hours before the standing committee on June 10. The Bill had previously received consideration by national organizations and experts in the subject with which it is concerned and by those whose duty it would be to apply it if it became law. Forty-eight hours before it was to be considered by the standing committee the whole of the terms of the wording of the Bill were in effect changed . . . The standing committee completed consideration of the Bill at its second sitting on Wednesday, June 19. It did so without sufficient consideration because there was insufficient study of the new terms by the experts and outside bodies to which I have referred. The Bill as amended is now before the House, but the Government have yet again tabled a whole series of amendments. The amendment list before us totals 36 amendments. They are amendments of substance and were tabled only yesterday – indeed, two of them became available to Hon. Members only this morning.

Mr Alexander Lyon, Minister of State at the Home Office, expressing his sympathy with Mr Stanbrook, explained that the matter he raised arose largely because the sponsors had been given the assistance of draftsmen and officials in redrafting the Bill in a confined period of time. Furthermore industrial action by the Government's printers had not helped the position greatly. Mr Stanbrook was not to know, however, that the Bill was yet to see even more changes before it received the Royal Assent, changes which fundamentally altered the operations of this measure.

Some doubts

Of the three objections originally voiced by the Justices' Clerks' Society the first two were removed in substance if not in theory by emasculatory emendation in the House of Lords, while the last was met altogether by the exclusion of criminal proceedings from the ambit of the Act. Nevertheless, two objections to the Act still remain which are of substance: it adopts an objectionable method to secure its end and it is unworkably complex.

As the Justice report remarked:

> The principal difficulty which has faced would-be reformers in other countries is the unalterable fact that something which has once happened cannot afterwards be made to "unhappen". More than once, they have quoted Omar Khayyam:
>
> The moving finger writes; and, having writ,
> Moves on: nor all thy piety nor wit
> Shall lure it back to cancel half a line
> Nor all thy tears wash out a word of it.
>
> (One author adds that nowadays, when the moving finger writes, a dozen Xerox copies are likely to be made).
>
> The difficulty is fundamental, and it is logically impossible to overcome it. It follows that any attempt to put a person who has been convicted into the same position as one who has not will involve some degree of artificiality, or appear as an unrealistic device. But there are degrees of unreality, and our concern has been to devise a system which achieves our object with as little artificiality as possible.

The way in which it was proposed this should be done was described by the chairman of the Bar Council in a letter to *The Times* of 11 July 1974, as not merely seeking to suppress truth but actually to legalize and positively encourage lying. Mr Bernard Levin, writing in *The Times* of 12 July, was even less kind. Finally, there is the inherent difficulty in any legislation of this nature in justifying the giving of special protection to those who have been convicted of crimes while allowing free discussion of all other discreditable activities and even of acquittals. The Faulks Committee in its interim report on defamation, for example, saw no valid reason why those who have been convicted under the criminal law should be specially selected out of all those who misbehave for favourable treatment.

In anticipation of such criticism the Justice report had pointed to the attention which is paid in a criminal trial to conceal the defendant's record from the jury, the rule against hearsay which prevents a witness from giving evidence of the truth as he knows it and the need to rehabilitate offenders. Furthermore, the report argued, the measures which it proposed would not *compel* but merely *permit* the telling of untruths: "that will be a matter for their consciences". By contrast, Mr Alexander Lyon, Minister of State in the Home Office, was perhaps more forthright when he said in the Commons:

> Yes, I accept that what we are doing here is legislation in order that a man shall be able to declare that a lie is the truth . . .

adding on a later occasion:

> We allow that out of a greater sense of compassion for the man who has lived down his past and should be allowed to live it down. There is no other effective way.

But was he right? In the present writer's view there were, basically, two main areas which called for reform: the unnecessary mentioning of irrelevant convictions in the criminal courts, an admitted, if rare, defect which could have been dealt with by administrative guidance in exactly the way as has now been done, and what might be described as the de-criminalization, both in court and out, of old convictions.

Long before the Rehabilitation of Offenders Act, Parliament had recognized that certain sentences ought not to carry the stigma of a conviction, and legislation recently consolidated in s 13(1) of the Powers of Criminal Courts Act 1973 so enacts with respect to probation orders and orders of absolute and conditional discharge. It would have been a simple matter for the range of sentences governed by this provision to have been extended substantially. No doubt, as the Justice committee recognized, there would have been difficulties in the way of preventing questions being asked designed to circumvent the object of the Act, but it is hard to believe that the necessary safeguards need have been as confusing as those enacted in this Act.

Despite its shortness, the Rehabilitation of Offenders Act 1974 is a remarkably complex piece of legislation. The commentary in *Current Law Statutes* asserts that it is "generally marked by ill drafting". Certainly there are serious difficulties of interpretation even for the lawyer in many important areas. The Act's effectiveness depends upon the erstwhile offender being fully aware (a) of his status as a rehabilitated person and (b) of his rights thereunder, but finding out whether the ordinary petty recidivist has become a rehabilitated person resembles nothing so much as an act of genealogy, with the Criminal Record Office sheet replacing the family tree. This very complexity may be its undoing in that it must be feared that honest men will declare spent convictions unnecessarily through doubt and that the dishonest will omit to disclose anything with the excuse that they thought that they were rehabilitated.

Index